Keeping It Real

Copyright © 2021 Karlie Mitchell

All rights reserved.

Dedication

    This book was inspired by blessings, life changes, challenges, and obstacles. I would like to first thank Jehovah because He gave me the gift of writing. I was playing tug-of-war with several titles for my book, and I feel this title speaks for itself. I send appreciation to the family and friends who have encouraged me to continue achieving my goal. I wrote this book because we all can relate to situations we have faced in our lives. If you can relate to my words, you also understand that everyone goes through things. The outcome is learning from our mistakes and not to condemn ourselves for making those choices. We will continue to make choices in our lives that may or may not be at our best interests. I hope you enjoy taking this journey with me.

                                            Be Blessed

Contents

The Cards We Are Dealt
The Rut
Unforgettable (A Personal Memory)
The Root of the Problem – Know Your Roots
Forgiving to Forget
Love's Addiction
Fantasy World
Punishment
The Glass Heart
Your Word is All You Have…Act Like What You Say
An Innocence Robbed
Learning from the Past
Holding Cell
Seat Fillers
Too Comfortable
Everybody Wants to Be Loved
No More Freebies!!!
Friends to Associates
Always Wanting Who or What We Cannot Have
Authenticity
Second Place
Everyone Ain't You
Misunderstood
Faces of a Mistress
Personal Thoughts
POEMS by Karlie
References

The Cards We Are Dealt

Have you heard several times "I'm just dealing with the cards I've been dealt?" I never thought about situations in that way. I didn't ponder on life as a "deck of cards." If you think about it, our lives are decks of cards. The way we get around that is "how" we deal with those cards. We have the ability to maneuver the cards and get them in the right places, so they won't fall out of our hands. Sometimes things happen in our lives where we cannot control them. Control is another important aspect of life. I've heard that we should worry about the things we can control and not worry about the things we cannot control. Again, I never looked at my life in that manner, but it is the truth. We cannot control what anyone in this world says or does. We cannot make people like us, love us, or even respect us. The only thing we can do is like ourselves, love ourselves, and respect ourselves.

Most of the time when we do that it rubs off on others and they start to do the same. We must love ourselves in order to love someone else. Self-love is the best love next to God's love. Is it true you cannot love someone else without loving yourself? Why is it so hard to love ourselves? We dwell on past hurts and decisions we've made in our lives that cause us not to love ourselves. This brings us right back to dealing with the cards we're dealt. How we "deal" with our past determines what happens in the future. If you received a "bad" hand, that doesn't mean the rest of your life will be that way. Sometimes we must move the cards around several times to get them where they need to be. Now, let's talk about loving other people. Let's face it some people make it very hard to love them. It could be their attitudes, disrespectfulness, or personalities. Love has a way of knocking you down. Sometimes when you think you've found love something always sabotages things. Guess what? Those are the cards being dealt. Love is

supposed to be peaceful, kind, and never fail. A lot of people do not feel that way about love. I, myself, feel love sometimes hurts. When you love someone, you love him or her. You put a lot of effort into pleasing that special person. One thing I've learned is that it's the "little" things that count the most. It doesn't matter if you buy all of the material things in the world. That's all they are...things. If you're dealt a good hand in life, I suggest you hold on to it. If your hand is not so good then make it better. You can add cards or you can take some away. If you want to start over, lay the old cards down and pick up a new set. Dealing with the cards in your life isn't always easy, but it can be handled in a way that will make life a little better. There is another way of dealing with those cards we're given in life. The word is called changes. Can we deal with the changes in our lives? The question is not "can" we deal with those changes.

    The question is "how" we're going to deal with them. We're imperfect humans and it's hard for us to handle those "monkey wrenches" that are thrown at us. At times it's hard for us to accept the situations that we are in. You may sometimes ask yourself "what am I doing" or "what did I just do?" When you ask yourself those questions, it's time to readjust those cards again. I'm learning that life is all about lessons. What you get from those lessons is what you will use throughout life's situations. The cards you're dealt is given to you by God but not always. The anxieties in life are based on the decisions we make. Most cards are your children, job, husband, wife or significant other, and other family members. You must make sure the most important cards are first. Faith is what keeps us going. Even though it's hard to keep faith in our lives, it's the way to receiving blessings. Faith is the key to a successful life whether you're single or married. Anything is possible for those who believe. That's a strong statement because this involves someone who is more powerful than any human on this earth…God.

These are critical times hard to deal with and God is the only one who can change things. You know sometimes it's so easy to SAY you have hope or faith but showing you have faith is completely different. There is a scripture in the book of Hebrews that states "faith without works is dead." I truly believe if you don't show you have faith your words are worthless. If you don't have any faith, then what are you working towards? A good question to ask ourselves is "Do we have faith?" If so, are we showing God we have faith in him? There is so much negativity in this world that it almost seems impossible to have faith. The Bible states these are "critical times." When you have faith, you love yourself and others more freely. You can see things more clearly. Life seems more manageable, and you appreciate what you have. Let's talk about "all things are possible to those that believe." This may be hard to believe for some people. When times are tough, it's hard to think about anything being "possible." It's almost like a domino effect...one thing after another until it finally stops. The domino effect is the endurance of the trial or trials you may be going through.

Another thing that's funny is how you live your life is the seed you plant. If you plant a bad seed, how do you expect it to grow? Do you think it will grow properly? No, if it's bad then you will reap what is bad. If it's good, you will reap what is good. God determines our heart conditions as to how the seed will grow. I've been told that when you receive God's Holy Spirit you will see things more clearly. Life will look clearer, and decisions will not be hard to make because you will put God first. This is how we all should live our lives. It's hard as imperfect humans to put God first but to have eternal life we must do this. I'm STILL learning when you want something it doesn't mean you will get it. The Most High makes those decisions for you. He determines if what you want is what you really NEED. Once again that's when God must be first in your life. Sometimes we yearn for something because we still have love or want to start a new life. The farthest thing from your mind is that you may not get another chance to start over. Why? I feel it's because you probably want things to work out in your favor so badly.

The Rut

I call this chapter "The Rut" because sometimes you get too comfortable around some people or your situation. Maybe it's someone you've known or lived with for several years. You get into this rut where you feel stuck. What does a person do when that happens? He or she should find a way to get out of that rut. A lot of times it really depends on what kind of rut you are in. This means you may be in an unfulfilling relationship, financial issues, family problems or instability. The rut is the situation you are unable to solve for whatever reason. Let us try to find a way to get out of the instability rut. This is just an example. You will have to do trial and error to find ways to solve your problem. You may have moved several times in the last couple of years. You are a single mom or dad, work a full-time job and may or may not receive support financially. You have moved from one place to another and even, perhaps, moved back to a place you have already resided. You notice a pattern that has developed. This pattern has to be changed because you begin to feel you have no stability in your life but especially your family. You start to contemplate ways to make everyone's lives stable again. We have to re-evaluate our priorities so we can make the necessary changes to become stable. One suggestion to resolve instability is to find a place where you and your family feel comfortable. You ask if the environment is safe, clean and accessible. As I said there are several ways to rid the rut of instability. You are the only person who can make that decision but use God as your guidance. As a matter of fact, pray about your situation. Pray incessantly. You may also have several "ruts" going on in your life.

In the beginning of this book, I stated our lives are like cards. We have to play the hand we are dealt but all of that stems from our choices. The book of Matthew says we "reap what we sow." It is about the seed we plant. If we plant a bad seed, we cannot expect it thrive. If you are in a relationship whether you are married or not, if it's not thriving then it's dead. The rut is your relationship is dying and you and your partner have to find ways to keep it alive. This only works when BOTH of you want to MAKE it work. A relationship is not a one-way street it consists of two people; therefore, they cannot go down a one-way. If there has been interference such as a third party, you will have to decide whether you want to continue the relationship or marriage. Once you pluck the root of the problem or "rut," you have to find a way to prevent reoccurrences. It is always easier said than done but we have to work at it. When you work, you show effort. It is always better to try instead of letting things fester or you may find yourself in the same predicament. This leads you to finding ways to get out of it once again. When you have gone through a lot of trials in your life, they become lessons to learn. It does not matter how old or young you are, you never ever stop learning. After a while, you WILL learn how to stop settling and start setting boundaries to prevent you from getting stuck. It is always about choices. We do not always make good choices but at the same time, our choices are not always bad. When making choices in our lives, we have to think ahead by imagining the consequences of the decisions we make. If we look forward to what the outcome may be, we will begin to choose wisely. It is not always easy because we want what we want.

We are imperfect humans who can be glutton at times. This means we can be greedy and bite off more than we can chew. Life is about choices and we have to think about who or what is involved. You have to look ahead BEFORE making the choice because this will allow you to think logically. If you know the consequences are beneficial and will not hurt anyone, you can feel confident you are doing the right thing. Sadly, oftentimes, we do things to benefit ourselves regardless of how it may hurt others. The bottom line is to **always remember that our choices always have consequences** IF we do not choose wisely.

Unforgettable (A Personal Memory)

Ever since I can remember, I loved being around my father. He was a good man. I remember when he used to work second shift and I was out of school for the summer. He would take me out to eat for breakfast almost every morning. We would go to the same restaurant each time. I loved the food there especially the pancakes. We would eat and talk for a long time. Afterwards, we would go to City Lake and feed the ducks. One day we went to the Lake and I was scared to get close to the ducks so he told me to get closer because they would not bite. He was taking pictures at the time. He was a great father. He liked to be neat and clean. I took that trait after him. I am a very neat and clean person. He always made sure his clothes looked good. He helped cook dinner and kept the house and yard looking nice. He did what a father and husband were supposed to do. As I got a little older, around 14-years-old, I learned my father had been living another life which led him to lose his job and we having to move.

Before we moved, he did get some assistance and afterward he was a new person. It felt good to have him back home. Even though we still had to move from our house, we remained a family until things took a turn. He was not able to get out of the lifestyle he was introduced to months back. We moved again but it was just me and my mama. We didn't see daddy for awhile, but he found his way back to us at some point. I never stopped loving him. His lifestyle made him choose a different path in his life which caused me to become angry. I asked myself why did he leave? I became even angrier when were put in stressful situations. Time went by and I saw less and less of him. I would see him at a store from time to time. He came to my marital reception, but only briefly. He stayed long enough to see his first grandson. I was pregnant with my daughter during that time. I'm not sure when I saw him again. He did see his second grandson at the grocery store some years down the road. I remember seeing him in the parking lot. I had my baby boy with me and he was so tickled to see him. He said, "He is so pretty." It felt good that he saw his grandchild but at the same time, I was still upset because he wasn't the same man I used to see years ago. I was also thinking about how we had not seen nor spoken to each other for a long time. Our relationship had changed drastically over the years. I was really hurt because I was his only child and he didn't make time to see his grandkids nor me. He didn't develop a relationship with them. I've realized that it takes TWO people to make a relationship work. I also did not do my part to keep up the relationship. My father was blessed because he had been in a terrible car accident some months before I saw him at the store. He was hit by a car while riding his bike. He was thrown 50 feet in the air. He survived a head injury. Sometimes you think people will change after something so traumatic, but it does not work for everyone. I think about 6 to 9 months after the accident he became very sick. He was admitted to ICU at the local hospital for massive hemoptysis. He was transferred to another hospital to have a procedure done. He did not improve after the procedure. I visited him while he was hospitalized. When his physician called the family to come to the hospital because of his 20% survival rate, all kinds of feelings went through my head. I cried on the way to the hospital. I kept thinking about how I wished our relationship had not taken a different turn. I thought about how my kids did not know him. They saw him a few times but that is it. They never spent time with him. When I arrived at the hospital, he was alert. He couldn't talk due to intubation. but he could nod. He was so happy to see the family especially me and my mother. I felt good because I thought he was on the way to recovery and we could start over. I had been thinking about how he could be that great father I used to know and become a great grandfather. I didn't visit him the next day because I felt confident he was getting better.

On June 14, 2006, I received a call from one of my father's doctor stating he passed away. I was shocked because of my hopes of his survival and his alertness. I could not cry after hearing those words. I drove to my grandmother's house to see my family. I went to the hospital to see him after he passed away. He looked so peaceful. All I could do was stare at him. Planning his funeral was very tough. It was hard because of all the mixed feelings that had been harboring in me for so long. I cried a lot during the funeral especially the viewing. I cried a lot right after his funeral and even months later.

I visit his grave at times to make sure the flowers are replaced and it is clean and neat. I tell him that I still love him and talk to him about what's going on in my life. Even though I cannot change what happened in the past, I will continue to keep his memories in my heart. I will always love him. My point is we are never promised tomorrow. We have to live for today and we must humble ourselves and pray.

Keeping It Real

The Root of the Problem – Know Your Roots

Do you ever wonder WHY? Why do people act the way they do? Why do they say the things they say? What goes on in people's minds? Your question is always WHY. The fact of the matter is we will never know why unless we ask. We may not always get an answer or the answer we are looking for but how else will we know. I have found there is always a root to a problem. The root is what's instilled in something or someone. You may have heard a person's childhood affects his or her adulthood. Personally, I think that's true. Sometimes, you have to look at the things you do or say and figure out where it comes from. For example, your parents never paid their bills or only paid them when they wanted to. Most of the time, this has an effect on the children as they get older and start working. When the kids get jobs, they may blow their money on unnecessary things instead of helping their parents with certain expenses or spending their money wisely. We see what our parent(s) do more than listen to what they say. Our parents are our roots as well as our grandparents and other ancestors. There are some people who do the exact opposite of what they are used to seeing.

When we become adolescents or adults, we may vow to ourselves NOT to spend our money unwisely or save what we earn. I believe we inherit certain ways

Keeping It Real

from our family members or shall I say parents. If your mother is or was an impatient person, you may have the same quality. You may not notice any of your "ways" until you are an adult. Your father may be or may have been someone who constantly cleans the house, the cars and especially his clothes. If you are the same way, most likely it's because you watched him and decided you will be the same way. We are all creatures of habits so when we see what our parents do or what other family members do it's common to do the same things…and continue doing them. Our ways are somewhat like genes. We inherit genes from our family members so our ways come from those genes. I'm not saying everyone grows up to be like their parents and family members. There are some ways of family members we do not care to adopt. If you see things you know that aren't right, you may have thought that's not the way you're going to live your life. Truth be told, we are our parents and family members because we share the same bloodline. As we get to know other people, we realize we do not have to be related to people in order to be a family. You can form better relationships with people who are not your family members. There are a lot of people who want to have close relationships with their families, but this is not always possible. We change as we grow older because of new friends, jobs, and other relationships.

    Now let's talk about those of you who have kids. Sometimes you may feel you have not done a good job raising your kids. It could be by the way they act or some of the things they say. Do you see any resemblance by their actions? Do you ever think "dang he acts just like me!" We do the best we can when it comes to raising our kids. When they succeed in almost everything, they put their minds to, you feel proud and happy. Even when they do things that are not pleasing you still feel okay. There are times you may look at the things your friends', family

Keeping It Real

members' and/or co-workers' kids do such as go to a known university or make a lot of money. You may hope the same for your kids. Sometimes we may feel like we didn't do a good job raising them but we have. We are not perfect human beings and all we can do is love our kids, talk to them, and teach them the right way. When they become adults, they will make their own decisions. As parents we can only do but so much at that point because they are grown. I'm sure you have heard or even been told to "let them go." A lot of times it's hard to let them go, but we must try. Just because we let them go doesn't mean we will stop thinking about their well-being. We can pray for them and help them as much as we can. We all make decisions that are good for us and the ones we love and sometimes we do not make good choices. We have to learn from the choices that aren't good and make the best of the ones that are beneficial.

Forgiving to Forget

It is very hard for humans to forgive AND forget the things people do to us. If someone hurts us, we are supposed to accept the apology and say all is forgiven. In reality all is not truly forgiven because we never forget that we were hurt. When we forgive the person, we get back the power that was taken from us. We also have to keep in mind how God always forgives us. He constantly forgives us for every wrongful act or inappropriate thought. If we don't forgive and forget, we will not be forgiven. We are all guilty of keeping a count of the injury that we received. The Bible states that we should not keep an account of the injuries we receive from others. I'm sure a lot of us are guilty of bringing up past hurts at times. The question is **why** do we dwell on the things that have hurt us. We are imperfect creatures; therefore, it may be hard for us to freely forgive. Sometimes it doesn't matter how long ago the situation happened. It could be three months or 3 years and we allow the same agonizing pain to linger. I'm sure you've been told several times if you forgive you will be free of the hurt and pain. We can enjoy life and start loving ourselves again. When we live in the past, we cannot move forward. If we can't get past what has happened, we won't be able to move on. It's definitely not easy to forget about painful situations, but it can be

Keeping It Real

done.

The key to forgetting is time. It takes time for everything whether you're waiting at the doctor's office or in traffic. It takes time to forgive and forget but it's not supposed to be that way. We are supposed to quickly forgive others as God quickly forgives us. If you're constantly trying to figure out why you were hurt, you may not ever get the answer. It seems if we knew why things happened the way they did, we would feel better. Some people think if knowing the reason why may help make the process a little bit easier. Does it really matter WHY we were hurt? Some people may say "yes" it does matter. The next question is what are you going to do if you find out the reason you were hurt. Can you do anything about it afterward? I would say the answer to that question is no. Some may feel differently by getting revenge but vengeance is not for us. We all have to work on forgetting after we forgive. It's easy to say "I forgive you" or "I accept your apology." We really don't think about forgiving also means forgetting. We are guilty of saying we forgive someone but continue to dwell on the hurt and pain.

When we dwell on the past hurt, we become angry. We become angry with ourselves for allowing the person to hurt us. There are times when the people who hurt us make it hard for us to forgive them because they constantly do the same thing over and over again. He or she will keep turning that knife they first inserted in our backs. It doesn't matter how many times the person has hurt us. It's the principle of the matter…we were hurt. It takes humility and prayer to accept what has happened to us. If it hurts it feels like a lifetime to get passed it. We seem to forget about the positive things because we focus on the negative. Life is a roller coaster and we have to learn how to deal with the ups and downs and the twists and turns.

Keeping It Real

Do you ever wonder when you will get your life together? Or do you wonder if your life will ever be "normal?" What is normal? We live in an imperfect world and surrounded by imperfect people. As I said earlier, we cannot make people treat us with respect, be our friend, or even like or love us. Everyone handles hurt differently. Sometimes it takes everything in us to get through one day. It can sometimes take every second or minute or hour to get through it all. One thing is for sure you will get over it. The key is to keep yourself from constantly getting hurt.

Love's Addiction

When we are addicted to something or someone, our minds, bodies, and lives are controlled. We breathe this person or thing all of the time. It's almost like we cannot make decisions without depending on our addiction. Love is like a drug. We use love to cover over transgressions such as disrespect, lying, or cheating. We can become addicted to people especially the ones we love. We will do any and everything for the ones we love when we're addicted. It doesn't matter how he or she treats us. The addiction is more powerful than any disrespect or bad treatment. For example, we will say a person is addicted to his spouse or significant other if you will. This person can be one of the most disrespectful, arrogant and selfish buttholes in the world. Yet, he or she can be the sweetest person. In this case, I'll say this person is more disrespectful than sweet but you love him or her very much. There are certain situations that have come up that have been more than you can bear for so many months or years. You are tired of dealing with this person so what do you do. You find a way to break the addiction. You find a way to get back your sanity, dignity, or life. Now, you have found a way to withdraw yourself from the drug. What's next? You are now in a place in your life where you do not want to be alone. You want someone or

Keeping It Real

something to fill that void. For instance, you meet someone who SEEMS to be a caring person. This person is very interested in YOU or so you think. You want to get to know him or her even though you turn a blind eye to the fact the person shows no interest. The funny thing about the situation is that this person PURSUED YOU. You were asked to go to dinner, a walk in the park, or lunch and you realize, after a couple weeks have gone by, that the two of you haven't been anywhere. You haven't even been to McDonalds! The picture is becoming clearer that you are the giver and not the receiver. Have you ever been a situation like that? It's called being MISLEAD! That can be a serious pet peeve. No one wants to be told a bunch of bullshit when the person who is handing it to you knows he or she will not be doing anything for you or with you. I'm sure you have heard someone has thrown up the smoke screen. Eventually, the smoke clears and you see the REAL person. It's quite sad how some people take advantage just to get what they want and then don't want anything else to do with you until it's convenient. Usually, the void is not completely filled because either that person doesn't have the same effect as the drug you withdrew from or he or she is worse than the drug. When things do not work out, sometimes you have a relapse. You end up using the drug again because you feel there is nothing else. You start to use that drug again and now you're hooked AGAIN. This time you get a slightly different effect and you like it. The problem is that it doesn't last long. Now you're back in the same rut you were in before you broke free. What can you do this time around? You can break free again. You already KNOW you can leave that drug alone because you've done it before. Eventually, you have a pattern of withdrawing and relapsing. The key is to break the cycle. You have to get off the merry-go-round. If you do not get off the merry-go-round, you will drive yourself insane. Let's not forget the ones who say they are not just physically attracted to you. Majority of the time, they ARE just physically attracted to you and just want some sex. They will do pretty much all of the things a girlfriend or boyfriend does in a relationship until they get what they want. Sometimes it can a close friend you have known for years. You have confided in this person and been yourself around him or her. He or she has even wanted to meet you places where NO ONE will see the two of you such as a hotel. Again…MISLEADING!!!

The love addiction takes control of our minds just as a person who is addicted to drugs or alcohol. You must WANT to break the addiction. You must ask yourself can you handle the withdrawals, per se, of ending the addiction. It's possible to have severe withdrawals just like a narcotic. Love is the drug that has the most powerful addiction. Love is so powerful and addictive it will have you doing things you shouldn't be doing such as cheating and have extramarital affairs. When we are in love or think we are in love, we use our hearts and not our brains. We know it's wrong, but we do it anyway. Sometimes we will even think God sent that person to us. We want to believe that person came into our lives to stay but we won't know if it's true until you see the signs. If he or she wants to have a future with you, that person will do all he or she can to stay in your life. Some people are there for the time being or temporarily. Some people just want you to be their therapist, sex partner, and maybe go out on dates every now and then. These types of people have NO intentions of leaving their home, wife, and kids. They will tell you all day every day that they are leaving and know damn well they are not going anyway. Some are truly there for the long haul because they know you are their future. They know you are the best thing that's happened to them. They know you have their backs when needed. Again, you will not know until you SEE. God created His children to love one another. He doesn't want us to hate each other but what do you do when the "love" drug is someone who does not respect you, cherish you, or treat you with decency. You have been using the drug for so long it seems impossible to let it go.

As I mentioned before, time is the only way to beat the addiction. We also must love ourselves enough to know we do not deserve the treatment we are getting from the drug. It's about moving forward. It sometimes takes a long time to move on but we must take it one day at time. There is a Tyler Perry movie about a woman who was basically addicted to love. She had been with her husband since they were dating in college. While in college he cheated on her and she went off. She drove her jeep into his RV a few times to knock it over. She was in a fit of rage because he didn't call her for two days. Her intuition told her to drive to his place to see if another female was there. She sat in her jeep for an hour, but didn't see anything until she was about to drive away. She was horrified to see a woman in the window.

After forgiving him after he begged her to, she took him back and continued to believe his lies. She put up with his disappointments and not working to help her pay bills until one day she snapped again. She thought he cheated on her again, but this time he really didn't. She didn't believe him and she was fed up. She divorced him even after he begged and pleaded not to. After he finally accepted she didn't want the marriage, he signed the divorce papers and compensated her for all of the money she spent all of those years and then some. She thought about how unfair she was to him and tried to reconcile the marriage, but it was too late. He was engaged to another woman. The same woman she caught him cheating with when they were in college. The love for this man she had for so long turned into HATE. She stalked their social media account and followed them. She became obsessed to the point where a restraining order was taken out on her and tried killing him. The moral of the story is things are not always what they seem. Love is supposed to be patient, caring, trustworthy, and kind. When a person is betrayed but does not know how to handle it, his or her thinking becomes warped. The heart is broken and it's hard to heal after being hurt. Love can be an addiction. We have to pray not to love or hate the "drug." It's going to be hard because it has taken a long time to get "addicted." The addiction didn't happen overnight and will not go away overnight.

We must re-evaluate our lives and replace negative things with positive things. There are other ways to be addicted to love such as being addicted to the idea of love. You may choose men or women who treat you badly and then move onto someone else who shows you a behavior that is totally opposite. You may choose someone who is clearly not available but he or she treats you a lot better than the previous person, so you stick around to see what happens. You KNOW this person isn't available but he or she doesn't disrespect you.

Fantasy World

We all grow up wanting to be something or somebody special. We may want to be an actor or actress, play professional sport, write a book, travel the world, or marry our king or queen. Some of us are fortunate to live out our fantasies and some are still trying to fulfill them. Some of us are not that fortunate. We go through our personal lives and get married, have a family and then we end up divorcing. We have marital problems and condemn ourselves. We sit back and look at our lives and see that it didn't turn out the way we wanted it. We are still living but not the way we thought. We look at movies that have this storyline where there are two best friends since childhood. Sooner or later they realize there are feelings there and one thing lead to another but know it doesn't help the friendship. They decide it's not the best thing to pursue but somewhere down the line they end up together anyway. In between all of this, one of them got married but ended up with the childhood friend. You hope that you find the person you have always wanted. Sometimes friends need to be that way… just friends because it can be ruined. Everyone wants to be loved. You look back and see that you got married but things didn't work out. You don't give up. Some people say they will never get married again. If you say never it means you've given up, you can't do it anymore.

We have our spouses, children and other family members but may still feel lonely. You can still be alone. It's not that you NEED to have someone in your life. It's that you WANT someone in your life. You want to grow old with someone and travel with that person. The kids grow up and go to college. Who is left in the empty nest? You. I commend these couples who have been together for 30, 40, 50 years or more. This brings me joy because there is respect for couples who have been together for so long. Someone once told me it's more about compatibility than love. Some people look towards compatibility than love. Some people think with their hearts instead of their brains. I feel that's what this person may have been trying to say. Love can be overrated at times because it's a feeling. When we feel, it's from the heart. You don't feel with your mind. The compatibility part comes into play when it comes to the mind which in turn has to do with the personality. Everyone wants to be loved no matter what.

When people go through things in life especially when it comes to relationships, we tend to hide our feelings. We sometimes go back to the fantasy land where we have already imagined living with this person and getting married. We imagine having kids and/or combining your families together if the two of you already have kids. We have already committed ourselves to these people and haven't known them for long. The good part about it is you SEE yourself with this person beyond the dating stage. You see more and you want more. You're seeking love and sometimes will do anything to get it. I talked about this in the Love's Addiction chapter. We look past all the flaws and red flags. We all have flaws and should try to correct them. The red flags should be yanked as soon as they go up. We tend to settle and hope for the best instead of being patient. I feel it's not a good idea to live life as a fantasy because you will not be able to deal with what's in front of you...REALITY. Sometimes it's hard to face reality because it's nothing but the truth. I'm sure you've heard "the truth hurts." Yes, the truth can hurt sometimes but not knowing is detrimental.

Keeping It Real

Punishment

When people hurt us, we tend to punish them. For instance, we may stop calling the person for a while, avoid them if we see them in public or act like they never existed. One situation is when someone we love or even like very much hurts our feelings. Let's start with someone you like very much. You can be as friendly as you want but if he or she doesn't want to talk to you it's not going to happen. I've come to the conclusion if you like or want to get to know someone it doesn't mean you will get the same response. Next, you love someone a lot and end up getting hurt. What do we do to the next person? We punish that person because we carry luggage from the previous relationship. We may build a wall around our hearts. Sometimes we play with the other person's feelings. Sometimes we may even fall in love with that person but act like it's no big deal. We make the person fall for us with no intention of "catching" him or her. We really make this person feel like they have gone crazy. Do you know what that's called? It's called misleading someone into thinking something is there when it really isn't. It's also called selfishness in a sense because you are reeling this person in because you like what you can get from them. Your needs are always met; when you need them they are always available even though you're not, and

Keeping It Real

face it you do like this person.

While we are doing all of this misleading stuff, we really end up hurting ourselves. We may hurt the other person but it's just temporary. In the end, we realize we should've given the friendship a chance because it could've turned into a fulfilling relationship. I feel we don't think about people come into our lives for a reason or for a season. I, personally, don't want just a season. I am sure most people want season after season and while and sowing and reaping something good at the same time. Some people come into our lives to restore not destroy. We want someone to come into our lives and stay there. Everyone has baggage called a past. We have to know how to keep it right where it is…in the past. We are supposed to learn from our past and not use it against others. Everyone is guilty of comparing his or her past with the next person. It's really not fair and we must learn how to stop pushing important people out of our lives. No one knows if you're ready to let someone "in" but you.

People will never be perfect but there are some who have good hearts or good intentions. We are not saints, but we do want to be loved, respected, or liked. One of the many things we have to learn is we cannot make everyone like us, love us, respect us or be with us. The result of us punishing the next person is losing out. When you finally get an epiphany, it's too late. Isn't that always the case? The person or people you pushed away are the ones you would like to have back or at least start over. When we make bad choices, we also punish ourselves. We feel guilty about the things we've done and for trying to make something happen that's not there. We hurt when we hang on to what we've done wrong or what someone else has done. You can be angry when you see that person or talk on the phone. Who is losing sleep though? The other person surely isn't. Nine times out of ten YOU are the one losing sleep over something that really was out of your control. He or she is moving forward but you are stuck in one place. It doesn't matter how old you are you never stop learning. We learn by trial and error because that's life. We go through so much when it comes to relationships whether it's family-related, work-related or personal. There are some people who will not change and continue to hurt you but only if you allow them to. We have to remove ourselves from those people and not punish others. We have family members who may have hurt us when we were 5 years old. We fast forward 25 years later and we are still talking about it at the family reunion. What are we doing? We hold on to things that don't really matter anymore. We have to let it go. We spend most of our time at our jobs. Have you ever noticed? When one of our coworkers does or says something that hurts us, we have to resolve the problem and move on. We shouldn't treat other employees the same way we have been treated. They are just innocent bystanders who have no idea what's going on and half of the time do not care.

The point here is we can't punish others for our past hurt and pain. We will never move on or have future relationships if we continue doing that. It's very important to treat people well. There are some who will not give a care what they do to anyone even when you've done nothing wrong. This type of person KNOWS he or she has done wrong but will rationalize and try to justify why. While they are rationalizing you end up being the one to blame. Have you ever known someone who was used to being treated a certain way and don't know what to do when someone treats them better? The person who I'll call the defendant gets moved to the back burner until the plaintiff realizes they are no longer in harm's way. It sounds crazy how you wouldn't want to give someone a chance to treat you right. We get accustomed to being treated a certain way and start to believe we're not worth getting treated differently. We are still convicting the defendant for something he or she hasn't done wrong. It's not fair but I feel we do this out of fear. Someone shared something with me about FEAR. This person received this information from a sermon. Fear is a False Experience Appearing Real. It makes a lot of sense to me. We fear something that hasn't even happened.

Punishment
Your past has come into the present
What am I to do
My hands are tied because of your holding back
I reach out to you just to be pushed away
Now I'm faced with should I go or stay
It's not fair to the one who only wants to love
The one whose heart is crushed to pieces
Do you realize you are hurting the one who care
The innocent bystander is who I am
Always getting blindsided and unaware
The only thing that's left to do
Is continue praying for a peace of mind
Ask God to tame those disquieting thoughts
Let him renew your broken heart and take away distress
Have faith in our Father because he always knows best

Keeping It Real

The Glass Heart

In order to know what a glass heart is, you probably have gone through trials in your life that affected the heart. The Bible says "the heart is treacherous who can know it." (Jeremiah 17:9) If anybody knows our hearts is the man above. When I speak of a glass heart, it's figurative. I'm referring to a broken heart. We know that glass is very fragile. It can easily be broken depending on the thickness of it. If you have strong feelings or they get hurt easily then you have a fragile heart. The "glass" that protects your heart can be easily broken. On the other hand, if you're the type where it takes a lot to hurt your feelings, or you always guard it then your "glass" is thick. It will take an army to break it. I guess you can say you're tough. Once the glass is broken it's pretty hard to mend. If you have the thick glass, it may not be hard to put back together because you can "glue" it. It may not take long to "bounce" back. A fragile heart usually takes a while to piece back together. Sometimes you have to put each piece back one at a time. Whether it takes one day, one month or one year, you are the only one who determines this. There are times in your life where you feel your heart will never stop breaking. You slowly glue the pieces back and you're fine for a while.

Keeping It Real

When things in life seem like they are looking good, one day the glass gets broken again. After a while it gets to a point where you can't glue it again. You're exhausted from the pattern you keep following. You're tired of the merry-go-round and want to jump off. Your next step is to find a solution. You have to find the reasons you continue getting your heartbroken. The root of the problem is YOU. I say YOU because it's a domino effect. It's the same thing right after another. The only person who can change this is YOU. We can treat people well and do the right things but for some reason or another you still get hurt. Your significant other decides things are moving too fast; his or her feelings came into play when it wasn't on the "agenda;" or the "needs" were met and no longer wanted. I'm just being honest because we all have to face heartbreak at some point in our lives. I've realized there are always signs when you feel something isn't right. They are called red flags. Sometimes things start to unravel gradually or even suddenly. A lot of times we see what we want to see which is perceived as an illusion. We know in our hearts that things aren't looking good but we push those thoughts aside because we don't want to face the truth. We are still learning and we will continue to learn until we leave this world. We have to endure this thing called "life" which was given to us as a gift. We must deal with different attitudes and personalities because we are imperfect. With that being said, there is a very big difference as far as how men and women deal with being hurt. Most of the time women go through the motions and bounce right back. We get passed the pain by talking to or hanging out with our girlfriends or finding things to do to detour those feelings. Usually, men keep those feelings inside and hardly ever portray they are hurt or have been hurt. There are some who will tell you they've been hurt and some will show you. Both men and women will sometimes guard their hearts and make it extremely hard to get through the front door. When someone else comes along, that person may go through the back door. He or she must go through the basement, up the stairs, through the back door, down the hallway, and finally the front door. We have to learn how to love again and it's okay to take your time. You may feel vulnerable because you've been hurt so many times and want to feel love and be loved. It's okay to be "cautious" because everything in this life is a risk especially a relationship. You will never be able to control the actions of others but you can control your feelings so protect your heart and limit who goes near it. We have to depend on God when we are lowly in heart. He always has His hands on us.

A Glass Heart
A heart isn't made to be broken
A heart should be full of joy
What can you do when it's constantly shattered
How do you mend the broken pieces
Each piece represents a painful wound
You patch them up so they can heal
With hopes of no one opening them again
A glass heart is something you never want to have
So guard it as much as you can
To avoid having to put the pieces back together again

Keeping It Real

Your Word is All You Have...Act Like What You Say

This chapter is dedicated to anyone who is tired of the mind games and wants to be serious. One thing you should know is most people do not like to play games. I'm sure some of you have figured this out already. It's hard to tell a lot of times because that's all it ever is...a game. When you tell someone you are not interested in a relationship, don't want to get attached, don't want to hurt anyone nor get hurt, call him or her your "girlfriend or boyfriend" but turnaround and do the opposite of everything you say, this is where trouble begins. The word is called misleading. When you mislead someone, you "lead in a wrong direction or mistaken action or belief often by deliberate deceit" according to Merriam-Webster's dictionary (Merriam-Webster Dictionary, 2016). You are saying one thing and doing another or doing one thing and saying another. When we meet someone we already know if that person will be a "rental" or a "mortgage." We already know if we are going to be platonic friends or "friends with benefits." Lately, the latter is what people do because no one wants to take responsibility for someone else's feelings.

When you deal with someone you are interested in, it can be like walking on eggshells so to speak. You have to watch what you say and how you say things to that person. Everyone doesn't have that tough skin and everyone is not sensitive either. People listen to the words you say and match them with the things you do. A red flag pops up when the two of them do not mesh. This is especially true for those whose trust has been broken. It's like making a promise you probably know you're not going to keep but you say it anyway. For instance, you promise this person s(h)e doesn't have to worry about you cheating. The point is if you really and truly mean it. If you can't trust yourself not to cheat then don't tell someone you will not do it. Another example is always telling someone you will call back and never live up to it. We are all guilty of this for some reason or another. It's either we know deep down we are not going to call back or we get distracted and forget. The eyebrow-raiser is when this person has a habit of doing it and without remorse. It's no big deal because they are constantly busy or into something so it should be "acceptable."

Another issue is someone who is misleading and know they are doing it. They will continue doing it as long as its allowed. The moment you call them out on their shit is when they change. Some people like to have their cake and eat it too by keeping their hands on you per se until the other situation doesn't work out. Say that you are interested in someone who surprisingly says he or she is also interested in you. As a matter of fact, this person is very interested in you. Yet you are not asked any questions about how you grew up, your family, kids, favorite color or food. YOU are asking all of the questions because you are truly interested. On top of that, you haven't been asked out on a date yet and it's been almost a month. This is just figuratively speaking. Is that person really interested in anything about you? Hell no!!!! What do you do now? Do you get upset or angry? Do you say anything at all? Some people may be like "she isn't even

Keeping It Real

worth it" or "yeah let me clear the air." I have heard so many times how silence speaks loud. It speaks so loud that within a few months down the road you will get a phone call or text from the one who let you get away. Mark my words…they ALWAYS come back! So, when your words don't match your actions, you are wasting other people's time. The point is to stop the talking and do the walking. If you don't be about it and then don't talk about it.

> "Your beliefs become your thoughts,
> Your thoughts become your words,
> Your words become your actions,
> Your actions become your habits,
> Your habits become your values,
> Your values become your destiny."
>
> — Mahatma Gandhi

Keeping It Real

An Innocence Robbed

There was a child who was very young but innocent as the day of birth. This innocence was taken from a child at an early age. You have to watch who you bring into your home because everyone cannot be trusted. You think some people are able to uphold your trust, but you find out in a short time it means nothing. I want you to imagine being at your job while your child is with the babysitter. The babysitter is at your home. You have to keep in mind you trust your babysitter. You go home for lunch one day where you find your bedroom door is not only closed but locked. You knock on the door and tell whoever is in the room to open it. It takes a minute for the door to open. You see your child sitting on the bed and the babysitter coming out of the bathroom. You ask what's going on and why was the bedroom door locked. Your child didn't say anything but had a suspicious look. Your babysitter tells you the door was locked to keep the children from coming into the room while she was using the bathroom. Supposedly, the kids kept trying to open the bathroom door.

The question you ponder on is why was the bedroom door locked? It didn't make any sense. You sternly let your child and the sitter know that your bedroom is off-limits. On your way back to work, you are not happy with what

Keeping It Real

you saw and needed more answers. You call the kids' mother or father to tell what transpired. It was agreed things sounded suspicious. You both agree to discuss the situation after work. The both of you speak with the child to find out what really happened. Your child feels more comfortable speaking with dad. Dad tells you that your child was forced to do sexual type things with the babysitter. This further confirms your suspicions. You knew it was something but unsure exactly what. You two decide to confront your babysitter's parents. You call the parents to fill them in on what has happened. They arrange a meeting for the following day. During the meeting, the parents ask the babysitter what took place. There are no answers to the questions being asked so you ask your child. As soon as the child answers, the babysitter finally talks. You find out this has happened on more than one occasion. Your child is stating several times significantly higher than the sitter. You are so angry at this point you are unable to cry. The sitter sits at the table silently crying, but you feel no remorse at all. As the discussion goes on, your babysitter's mother questions your child the difference between right and wrong. You tell Ms. Mom your child probably felt it wasn't wrong since the sitter is a lot older and was in charge. The babysitter was asked "why" but again no answer. Ms. Mom decided the reason for this unacceptable situation was due to curiosity. Are teenagers curious when it comes to taking advantage of a child? You are asking yourself this at that moment. You become angry after hearing the justification for the babysitter's actions. The resolution to this problem is no more babysitting and to move on. It, the situation, still doesn't sit well with you. You talk about it later and for another day or two. After a month goes by, you talk to Ms. Mom again. You discuss counseling for your child and you suggest she gets counseling for hers. She stated if you get counseling for your child, does her child need to sit in on the sessions. You state sessions for her child not both together. She agrees to counseling and asked if you would inform her when to get started. Later that day you discuss your conversation with your spouse. The counseling was never scheduled; therefore, everyone moved on with their lives. In the midst of it all, you ask your child how does the situation influence her? You're told it's a bad feeling and shameful.

As time goes by, you still wonder if your child will be "different." A couple of years or so go by and you ask your baby has what happened caused any anger issues. There started to be changes in behavior regarding anger. Your child remembers a little of what happened but not enough to discuss. You're concerned about your failing to seek professional help. You feel if you sought help it may have healed things. Even though there were no signs of "trauma" or stress, you're thinking later in life the memory will rear its head and your child may retaliate. This "thing" has been swept under the rug and forgotten. You know deep down it will never be forgotten. You will always remember what happened. After all this time you have suppressed your feelings towards the babysitter. It took you two weeks to tell your own mother because you knew it would badly hurt her. All is forgiven but never forgotten. According to the Bible, we are to forgive AND forget but it's not easy for imperfect humans because we have feelings. There is always something reminding us of our past experiences. We have to learn from what has happened and keep moving forward. Yes, it's definitely easier said than done, but we have to keep pressing on in order to be blessed.

Keeping It Real

Learning from the Past

I want to talk about this because there are a lot of people who dwell on the past and condemn themselves. For instance, you meet a nice man or woman somebody you're interested in and want to get to know that person but you've been hurt. Your heart has been broken several times and you're tired of getting hurt and you're scared. You have that guard up and then you start looking for signs or red flags per se in that person. You start wondering if this is going to be one who hurt me just like the other person or is this going to be a person who's going to respect me and treat me like I should be treated. It's a scary thing when you're meeting someone new because some of us will not admit it, but we want to love or want to be loved. Some people don't want to be alone, or it would not bother them, but I feel the majority of humans do not want to live their lives alone.

When you meet somebody it's probably somebody you want to be long-term with. You have to learn to keep that luggage where it should be…in the closet. We learn from our past we are not supposed to punish the next person. It's not fair to them but you do have to protect yourself as far as your heart is concerned. Me, personally, I'm still learning. I'm still scared. It takes time but the

Keeping It Real

biggest word here is trust. We are imperfect humans and someone once told me that we are creatures of habit. I agree that we have habits, both good and bad, that we are so accustomed to. It really is a kind of weakness especially the bad ones. I've heard the saying "once a cheater, always a cheater." I feel that may be true but not all of the time because there is something called change. People can and do change if they truly want to. It may depend on the stage they are in. When you get in your late 30s and 40s, you would think some people would want to be stable or want to settle down.

Unfortunately, it doesn't work for everybody. Some people in those age brackets want to settle down and not play games. We must think about trusting people who we allow to come into our lives. The other word is faith. Trust and faith go hand in hand when you place them in God's hands, continue to pray about it, and put that trust in the relationship or beginning of one and hopefully it will work out in your favor. Sometimes we have to face the fact that it doesn't work out. God removes this person, and we wonder why. A lot of times we already know the reason why. We see the signs but ignore them or turn a blind eye. They are also called RED FLAGS. Yes, red flags have been mentioned several times in this book. When you see these flags, you're supposed to run but a lot of times we have the heart that give people a benefit of a doubt. We decide to give this person a chance or chances. We sometimes give them too many chances and this can be frustrating because you're thinking you may be naïve for continuing to allow the person to get away with stuff. You have to realize whose worth fighting for because some people are not worth the fight. You may also notice the other person is not fighting for you or showing that you are important. This is definitely a red flag but a lot of times we continue to give chances. Praying

Keeping It Real

about your past and asking God to keep your negative thoughts quiet, otherwise, you will dwell on it and investigate because you may start wondering why if he or she starts to act strange or different. Some people are workaholics and put their jobs and families before allowing anything personal to interfere. Sometimes it does not matter if that person is special, or feelings are involved.

Even though it may not seem to be fair, if you are grown, married, single, have bills, and have children, you have to work. It is about MAKING time! Some people may find it hard to look into the future because they are still stuck in the past. If you are still wondering why, you still do not have reasons to questions from your past, you will never ever be able to move forward. If you know deep down that what you are trying to pursue is positive, leave behind all of those what-ifs. You have to think about how the other person feels because it does matter. The point is there is a reason why the past is the past so forgive and move on. The past will drag you down. It is like driving but looking in the rearview mirror the entire time. How will you be able to drive safely if you are looking back? We are guilty of looking back at times due to regret. We have to accept what is happened and ask for strength and guidance.

Keeping It Real

Holding Cell

Did you know that we are prisoners of our actions? I mean when we do something and suffer consequences, we make ourselves prisoners. What does the state do with prisoners? They place them in a cell for a certain amount of time until released? Imagine someone in a holding cell for reasons that were not his or her fault or maybe it was a fault of theirs. If you have ever experienced sitting in a holding cell, you know how agonizing it is. Your new enemy is named "waiting." You feel that you are being held against your will (when it is not your fault.) You sit in this box with a chair, maybe one or two windows, and a heavy-duty locked door. The sound of the door makes you jump each time it closes because it is very loud. It only locks from the outside which makes you feel even more trapped. You sit on this hard chair and all you can do is THINK. You wonder when you will be able to get out. You start to grow impatient because you are thinking about why you're in a place you know you don't belong. You watch people walk back and forth past your cell. Yes, it is YOUR cell while you're incarcerated. Every face you look at has no expression of sympathy because they (sheriffs and officers) deal with it every day. Your facial expression screams "get me out of here!" You constantly hear keys jingling with the hopes of someone coming to unlock the

Keeping It Real

door. No, it is the inmate next to you that is being released. Why not you? The reason is a process you have to go through in order to be released. The only thing you can do while you are locked up is contemplate, ponder, or think about everything. I mean everything that has gone on in your life up to this point. There is no book, magazine, or even a Bible to read. You may be fortunate to see a poster on the wall. You see that someone has engraved sayings on the glass window, so you try to read that.

Obviously, they were bored as you are with no pencil, pen, paper, coloring book, or crayons. Nothing! You constantly look at your watch. Every second, minute, and hour feels like a whole day. There IS something for you to do and that is pace the floor. As you see workers walking by, you wonder what goes on in their heads. Ah, you have figured out what they may be saying, "Just another member of society making bad choices." Even though YOU know you do not belong in that dreadful cell, the "outsiders" feel that you do. It does not matter because you are there, period. The keys jingle again but this time you are going to face the judge. You are adorned with accessories of handcuffs for the wrists and ankles and a chain around your waist which connects to the handcuffs around your ankles. Afterward, you are escorted to the courtroom. As you are walking down the hallway and up steps, the cuffs on your wrists and ankles begin to rub against your skin. You start to walk a little slower because it hurts. You are literally dragging your feet. The verdict is given then you are released. Yes, you can finally leave after being held for so long. Wrong! You are placed back in the holding cell until you are officially free. Remember when I mentioned there is a process? The paperwork has to go from this desk to that desk until its back in the proper hands. It's just like an assembly line where there are various stations so

Keeping It Real

you can imagine your paperwork being passed around. You are back in the holding cell once again but it's 10 times worse because you "know" you are free to go but you STILL can't go anywhere.   After a two hour wait, the keys jiggle and your door opens. By this time you are crying because you wasted a day full of nothing and you are angry. You walk out of the building exhaling. Now you have to figure out what to do next. Let us compare this to trials in our lives. There are so many trials we can talk about such as financial, personal, or work-related. All of them have placed you in a "holding cell" at some point. You were at a standstill until your solution released you. Someone once gave me a mental picture of the crossroads in life. We all reach a crossroads especially when it comes to decision-making. When you are unable to decide, you feel is difficult. You are pivoting. You really do not know which road to walk down so you turn this way and that way. You may have already gone down two of the four roads, so you are hesitant because those roads were "wrong ways." Now you are back in your holding cell again. We sometimes have to pump our brakes, per se, so we can think. Our holding cell confines us for a while. You know how your mama used to say, "get somewhere and sit down," that's what we have to do. The holding cell makes us ponder and come to reality. It can also make us feel we are going crazy because we may not be able to come to a solution on how to break free. When it comes to matters of the heart, our feelings are sometimes confined to the holding cell. We can fall in love with someone or get hurt and decide to keep our feelings bottled up. Eventually, it comes to a breaking point when those feelings need to be unleashed. The reason I wrote this chapter is because we all have been in a holding cell called life. It does not matter how young or old you are you will always experience some kind of trial while you're living on this

Keeping It Real

earth. We cannot change any human being in this world other than ourselves. When you have been handcuffed for reasons, you feel are not your fault, try to find ways to release yourself. One way to break free is forgiving the other person but the most important thing is to forgive yourself.

Keeping It Real

Seat Fillers

It seems everything in life is temporary these days. Everything IS temporary such as our lives here on earth, relationships, and jobs. I will start with relationships because a lot of people are in one. They are only temporary if you do not do the work to make them permanent. It does not seem anyone wants to be in a long-term relationship because of the benefits. We get benefits from doing little to no work for them. It is sad but we allow it. You may find someone who SAYS they want you or sees a future with you but really shows no action of it. This is called "talk is cheap" and that it is. You can talk until you turn blue in the face about plans with this person but have no intentions of doing anything you say. Again, YOUR WORD is all you have until the day you die. A lot of times we are with others until we so call find someone better or a seat filler. The saying goes "the grass is greener on the other side" or not. Well, the grass is not greener on the other side most of time. I saw a movie about questioning being married and one of the characters cheated on his wife to be with the "other side" who he found out was only giving him 20% of what he thought was missing in his previous marriage. My point is relationships are great but if you know deep down it is temporary for YOU then don't get involved with someone who wants to be permanent. When we continue to stay involved with someone who is not ready for

Keeping It Real

a relationship it is called settling. Some people may think when you settle with someone you may be desperate. This may not be true for everyone. It depends on that person's agenda. We know when things are not right. We know when the person in our lives is someone who will not be there "until death do us part." They are temporarily there and maybe using us as a bridge until they are tired of us or find someone who they want to be permanent with. The main thing is to know when they are a keeper.

Almost everyone knows what it takes to make a living and that's prayer and employment. You should always keep in mind that you can be replaced at any given moment. If you pass away tomorrow, you will be replaced the same day or very soon. You may have your job one day and literally the next day it is taken away from you. You should always keep your options open because you will never know what could happen. There are some people who have lost their jobs several times for reasons out of their control such as a layoff. Most of the time if you do your job, have good attendance and be prompt, you will have job longevity. I know sometimes even being a great employee does not mean you're incapable of losing your job. You have to thank God each day for your job and always pray you will keep it so you can provide for your family. I want to add how being a temporary employee is just a seat filler too. There are some employers who do not acknowledge their temporary employees and there are some who welcome them as if they are permanent. There are perks for employers when using temporaries such as saving money by not paying for medical benefits and vacation. When being a temporary employee, you have hopes of becoming permanent at some point? Who would not want to become permanent? You have to do your best and nothing less and those doors will be open for you. There are employers who will bypass you with experience and degrees for someone who is willing to accept a lesser pay. They need someone to fill the seat…period. The COVID pandemic has disrupted lives all of this world especially jobs. There were companies who had to shut down due to the pandemic. There were some places who were able to remain open during the pandemic. There were also companies who were not able to reopen due to profit loss. This resulted in job loss for so many people. Now there are plenty of jobs hiring due to lack of staff.

    Our lives are also temporary on this earth even though God meant for us to have everlasting life. We are imperfect humans and the choices we make, things that we do, and how we treat others plays a big part. Our bodies are temporary as well. We are fortunate to walk the earth and have everything that we need. We were provided this even though we did not deserve it. We have to be ready to accept God in our lives and have faith in the resurrection. When Jesus Christ is resurrected, we will be able to live in Paradise.

Keeping It Real

Too Comfortable

I named this chapter Too Comfortable because some of us are ungrateful and some are very appreciative. There are people who come into our lives who do not appreciate us. I know everyone is different, but it is not rocket science when it comes to being grateful. People come into our lives either as blessings or lessons. God brings people in our lives so we can give to them. The problem is that we are imperfect and take advantage of the person or people who give to us. Is it fair to take and not give? I know there are circumstances that may prevent us from giving to someone or giving back. Life is unfair sometimes, but we have to take the good with the bad. I, personally, feel unappreciated when I give my time, a gift or some positive reinforcement and I do not even get a "thank you." It tells me that my time is invaluable. One of the worst feelings in the world is to feel unappreciated. You feel that it is a waste of time…of YOUR time. There are some people who are just selfish. I have always heard that people who do not have siblings are spoiled brats. This may be true for some but not all people who are "the only child" are brats or selfish for that matter. Some are very giving and do not mind sharing things. I will give you an example of being "too comfortable." If you start treating someone a certain way in the beginning, then you should continue doing those things. Do you know why? The reason is that the person will eventually EXPECT you to continue doing those things. If you give that person too much, they may take advantage of it to the point where they will not do a thing for you. If you send morning and night messages every day to start with then that is something you should keep doing. The things we do to impress people are sometimes fake most of the time. We sometimes bend over backward to get what we want and change ever so quickly after we have received it.

When you stop doing what you were doing at first, you have gotten comfortable. It is OK to be comfortable but not in a way that it takes advantage of someone. I guess it is in our nature at times to get used to being treated a certain way. If you are around someone who always treats you well, you will always expect it from that person. We have to learn how to appreciate one another because you never know what the other person may be thinking. Some of us can give and not expect anything in return and others give with an agenda. Yes, at times, you would like a little something in return especially if you are always giving. It is really not fair to give and give but never get in the process. The message here is to always appreciate when someone helps you when needed or even if they do it "just because" they wanted to. There are a lot of people who have giving hearts. If you have people like that in your life, cherish them because they will not always be around. The point is not to expect anything from anyone here on this earth because you will get disappointed every time. Do you ever find yourself always being led back to where you started? You make the same mistakes over and over and over again.

There are several things on your mind, but it makes you go crazy. You become indecisive. Where are you? You are at a pivotal point. For instance, if you

Keeping It Real

have to choose between two job offers and they both are great offers, yet, you do not know which one to take. What is your next step? You have to look at the pros and cons of each job. Which one pays more and/or have the best benefits? Are they both located near your home? I am going to talk about the decisions we make in life. If you find yourself regretting decisions you have made, it's time to change your thinking. I am sure we've heard that plenty of times. Yes, that sounds weird. What I am trying to say is take a different direction towards your thinking process, but it's a difference between thinking and doing. There are so many people involved especially children and other family members. You have to consider your current job and expenses that may be incurred or possibly decreased. What is a pivotal point? Imagine you are walking down a gravel road and you come to an intersection. Which road do you turn? Do you keep straight? Turn left? Turn right? Go back down the same road? Sometimes we come back to the same situation repeatedly. Why? It could be because we were not comfortable with the first decision we made. It can also mean we did not consider the consequences. If we have consulted with God and weighed our options, we should be fine with the decision we have made. If you get backlash or a lot of opinions from others and you become discouraged, it may be hard for you to decide. We, sometimes, allow our family members and/or friends dictate our decisions in life.

Keeping It Real

Everybody Wants to Be Loved

I have heard that love is overrated and how some people take it out of context. In my opinion, love is love. Your actions show how much you care and LOVE someone. You can yell, sing, or whisper the word and it does not change anything. I think some people do not like to use the "L" word because it's like a "contract" to that person. If you tell someone you love them, you may be hooked. If you tell someone you love them, you'd better mean it because that is not something you toy with. You learn how to love someone based on how you were raised as a child. If your parents, grandparents, aunties, or uncles who may have raised you, I am sure they showed you love. Love is not overrated. When we have been hurt, we run from love. We do not want anyone to get close to us. We do not want to commit ourselves to anyone. We do not want to be bothered. We just do not. It does not matter how many times you may have been hurt or betrayed, deep down you still want to be loved. You do not want to grow old alone. You just don't want to be by yourself at all yet you still don't want to love. You want to love everything but the person you are with. You love yourself but no one else. I don't know everything, but I do know how to love someone. Women are the most nurturing creatures on this earth. God is love and His love is never ever overrated. His love is constant and without limits. Love is about actions.

Keeping It Real

If you show someone you love them, they will always believe you. If you say you love that person but barely show you love them, they will have zero trust. A lot of people believe in their eyes when it comes to feelings. We must have faith in our loved ones as well but along with that we have to see, hear, smell, and touch. When we use those senses, it seems that is our stamp of approval. This thing called love is beautiful if you do not abuse or take advantage of it. We may feel sometimes we will never love again after a broken marriage or relationship. We may not want to love after being physically, mentally, emotionally, or verbally abused. We may feel unloved when we are constantly rejected by others especially our loved ones or the ones who we loved but did not love us. It is hard to fathom why love can also be dangerous. It goes back to being abused in some form and the abuser still says he or she loves you. Love can also be harmful when jealousy is involved. Love is not jealous or envious. It is kind, nurturing, gentle, and caring. Sometimes the people we allow in our lives make us not want to love or be loved. Some people may treat us like we do not have feelings. If we continue to allow people to treat us that way, we are sometimes drawn to those types of people without knowing it. You cannot look at a person and assume he or she will love and respect you. We have to get to know this person first. I feel one of our biggest fears is to love someone who does not love us back. It has to be one of the most hurtful feelings. You spend time and get to know this person and eventually you become fond of him or her. After some time goes by, love creeps its way in. You can be with someone for years and find out later they either just cared for you or never loved you. It could be someone loved you and you did not love that person. Some people run from love like it is a contagious disease. We cover our hearts so love (the disease) will not enter. If love finds an opening in the heart, it will creep in. The key is will you allow it to manifest and cover you. Are you going to allow past hurt and pain to prevent you from loving this person back? As Teddy Pendergrass used to sing "It feels so good loving somebody when somebody loves you back!" He sure said that right! It does feel good when someone loves you back.

When you are in love, you have more pep in your step. When someone loves you back, YOUR world is okay and everyone around you SEES your glow. People see a "different" YOU when you know you are loved. It does not have to be about a relationship with the opposite sex. Being loved by your parents, siblings, and other family members, makes you feel good. Yet, when you know someone does not love you or find out you're not being loved, it makes you feel really bad. You have wasted your time putting energy into someone or people who could have cared less. Sometimes you may feel is it even worth treating people with kindness and love. We are supposed to treat people with love. You never know what a person's agenda is when you allow them into your life. You will always have to look at their actions. We tell each other "I like you a lot," "I care about you," or "I love you," but may not show it. You can tell someone all day long that you love them, but no one will believe you if do not do what you say. Love is kind, patient, and does not cause injury. We have to be careful with whom we give our hearts to because everyone does not care or have our best interests. There are people who have agendas. Their agenda is to get what they want from whomever they want. We must make sure we do not get used or taken advantage of. A lot of people have good hearts and some do not. If you are a giver, you will probably do all you can to help someone whether it is monetary, emotional, or physical. The ones that give are usually the ones whose hearts get

Keeping It Real

broken and taken advantage of. It is nothing wrong with helping others because that's what we are supposed to do. The problem arises when you see that your kindness is mistaken for weakness. It is like how a lion walks around searching for prey and once he (or she) finds what it is looking for…it pounces. That may be a bit extreme, but my point is some people will milk you dry to get what they want. You have to have your antennas up and be prepared. Someone mentioned that everyone wants to be loved, but everyone does not know HOW to love. I thought was a valid point. There are people who have loved someone and then changed just like you change your clothes for whatever reason(s) it may have been. There could have been a tragedy that occurred, but if you really love that person being it is a spouse, child or other family member, you shouldn't change how you treat that person because of your selfishness. Usually, what you put out is what you receive.

Keeping It Real

No More Freebies!!!

I titled this chapter No More Freebies because we find ourselves giving away too much to too many people and receiving nothing in return. Sometimes we receive little in return. This can be related to our bodies, whether it is a man or woman, money, our time, our love, our kindness, and our hearts. I will start with our bodies. Instead of starting with the women this time, I will start with the men. Believe it or not, men are used for their bodies too. It does not matter if it's the private part or the six-pack abs. Sometimes women just want to have sex with men and not deal with all the other drama that comes with it. The "other drama" is neediness, wanting to spend every waking minute with her, jealousy, the constant misleading of feelings, and sporadic text messages and calls. Sometimes women just do not want to be bothered. Sometimes women just want the "fix" and move on because they can do without anything else. Truthfully, some women do not NEED the "private part" because there are plenty and I mean plenty of "other" things and ways to get the "fix". It is a want unless she is a sex addict or nympho.

As far as the women, we give far too many freebies, and I am not just talking about the cookie. We give everything… our hearts, minds, souls, and yes, the dang cookies. Women sometimes give away the most precious and private

Keeping It Real

part of us before we even commit to a man. Sometimes that is where we go wrong but not all of the time. Lately, you may have heard some people say it's okay to have sex first because it will determine whether you want to continue having sex with that person or continue getting to know that person. I feel if a woman (or man) wants to wait to have sex until marriage, it is perfectly fine. If someone wants to do it before marriage, then it is that person's decision. The saying goes "to each his own." Women work hard and bust their behinds when it comes to love and so does men. Men and women both love hard and that seems to be where we get hurt. When we trust, we give it our all. We are nurturers and will go for broke if it is for our men and women IF we feel it's worth it. The freebies come into play when we give and give all those things away. We get lied to, cheated on, and used. When we really need something, he is not there for us. Most of the time, not all the time, women will only ask our men for something if we are in dire need. The biggest test is seeing if our men will have our backs when we really, really need him. If we realize our men are not there for us, we will start thinking about all, and I mean, everything, we've done for him and start to compare it to what he's done. It may not sound right but it is true. Women do not like to give their all and not get something in return. The little things make a big difference such as flowers or a card. Please do not get this twisted. I am fully aware men can and do go through the same thing women do when it comes to love. We ALL have to be mindful when it comes to relationships.

Keeping It Real

Friends to Associates

Have you ever noticed over the years your friendships changed a lot? The friends you have known for years are no longer in your life or they come and go. The besties are not even around anymore. I am sure you have heard the saying "Men come and go but friends last forever." That may not be verbatim, but I am close. It is true that men come and go, but TRUE friends last forever. We have friends whom we have grown up with and for some reason or another departed either because they moved away, or you moved on or found new friends. As you get older, you will see who your real friends are. You may come to realize that you were there just because you were needed. You may realize you were just a childhood or high school friend. You will forever be remembered and treasured. You may see that "your" friend(s) will hang out with their "other" friends and not you anymore.

It is normal for your friends to have other friends that you do not hang out with or don't know. It is just a matter of time when you will see you are only asked out for specific reasons or during specific times. One Friday night you get a call from your homegirl (or homeboy), whom you've known for a long time, asking if you and the kids want to meet him or her and the kids at the mall to go

Keeping It Real

shopping. Now, on Saturday night, you see pics of your home girl with her "other" friends at a local club. Where were you Saturday night? You were at home, alone watching TV or whatever. Did you get a call from your homegirl (or homeboy) asking if you wanted to go to the club? I have to be real about this because it has happened to everyone. What this may tell you is friends pick and choose who they want to go certain places with. You could be the "hang out with the kids" friend or the "go out to the club" friend or the "talk about my problems" friend. You might be the "just talk at work" friend or the "work wife or husband." What should you do? You should go out and meet new people and be okay with your friends meeting other people. It sounds simple, doesn't it? You should hang around friends who will have you around anytime.

    We do have busy lives and we understand that but having friends in our lives helps us get through those hard times. Our friends are our "go-to" people to talk to, eat or just laugh with. You must keep moving forward and just check in on your friends every now and then. There are going to be people they keep in contact with daily and you may not be one of those people anymore. We just have to deal with it...or not. I guess the key thing to all of it is not to worry about stuff that you cannot control. We must realize is the position we play in people's lives. You must know where you fit in. Once you figure it out you will know how to deal with others accordingly. For example, if you do most of the calling and/or texting, fall back and see what happens. There was a post on social media stating that some people are just friends and others are siesta-friends. It makes you think about your own friendships whether it's male and/or females. It goes back to knowing what position you play in peoples' lives. You could be thinking you are a friend-sister or friend-brother but you're really just a "friend" or "associate."

Keeping It Real

Sometimes you are not the go-to person anymore because you don't get updated on what's going on in your friends' lives anymore. I can bet you other people know more than you do. Some people keep their circles small and who could blame them.

    Again, KNOW your position in friendships. Also, know whom to be loyal. Loyalty is not something you just give to anyone. Most of the time you have to see how that person rolls. You need to know if you disclose information whether it's personal or business, you are not going to hear it elsewhere. You need to know if he or she will become a friend or just a what…associate. For instance, you give loyalty to the utmost to someone you consider a close friend but find out that person has been having diarrhea of the mouth. Someone warns you about this person telling others about your conversations with him or her. What do you do? You are fuming deep down inside, and it makes you want to confront that person. Should you do it or not? It depends on YOU. Some people may confront the friend and some may not. Everyone doesn't respond to situations the same way. You could change the way you deal with that person without showing giving a clue that you know anything. You can change your attitude without having an attitude if you get what I mean. Another scenario regarding friendships relates to the platonic. You have a platonic friend which is someone you hang out with and talk on the phone sometimes but nothing intimate. You don't kiss or have sex. On the other hand, you hang out with this person, communicate via text, talk on the phone, and basically act like a couple. You are friends but not exactly platonic. You have a misunderstanding, or the person that's misunderstood so the other person wants to "remain" platonic. You are not understanding because all you wanted to do was take things slow. You start to conclude that maybe you just weren't going "fast enough," therefore, not getting "physical." So, you are thinking this now platonic friend will still keep in contact with you but he or she doesn't. Actually, the behaviors started changing months prior. He or she doesn't text anymore, doesn't check on you, or nothing. As a matter of fact, your "platonic" friend acts like you do not exist at all. Yet, you seem to check on this person every now and then which is appreciated but he or she NEVER checks on you. You don't even get holiday texts anymore. My point is when someone wants to be platonic or changes the friendship status to platonic, it's basically means "we are not friends no more." Honestly, it's quite sad and downright messed up that you spend all of that time…months…with this person and now you are nothing to them. And guess what…you may feel hurt? Now, you have to act like you don't care. It may be hard because you may not be that type of person, but some people respond when you don't say not one word to them anymore. It just makes you mad when you are trying to figure out what went wrong and why that person didn't understand you.

A person that changes up that quickly after spending 6-8 months was NEVER your friend in the beginning. Maybe he or she had an agenda. Maybe he or she felt since you two were going out to eat, texting daily, buying each other gifts every now and then, that it would lead to something such as sex or relationship. We should enjoy the friendship part before getting into the relationship or having sex. You have to question who your true friend is and who isn't. Some people prefer to hang by themselves because there are others who choose to be messy. Yes, it's good to have that one friend or friends to hang with and will truly be there for you but at the end of the day all you have is YOU.

Keeping It Real

Always Wanting Who or What We Cannot Have

Why do we always want what we cannot have? I guess the reason is just that…we cannot have it. I do not feel that's always true. I feel it depends on the situation. I will give an example. You meet someone who you found out was married or in a relationship "getting ready to leave" his or her spouse or significant other. Yes, "married getting ready to leave his or her spouse" because that is what most will say. In the beginning, you two are just friends but as time goes by you develop feelings for each other knowing the marital or relationship status is just that…MARRIED or in a relationship. You continue following your heart because you have fallen in love KNOWING this person is unavailable. The two of you plan to continue the relationship because there are plans of moving out. You have faith in this person so you believe things will work out. A year has passed by then two, three, and working on another year and no change at all. You are in the same situation and so is your partner. There have been several reasons why this person has not moved out such as finances or the kids or fear. Yet you are still told things are going to work out. One day you finally have an epiphany and realize your spiritual life is at stake and you made a mistake. You knew it was wrong in the beginning, but you believed what you were told. What do you do?

Keeping It Real

You can pray and ask for forgiveness and try moving on. I am sure you've heard plenty of times, don't worry about something you have absolutely no control over. You have control over what YOU think, say and do. You do NOT have control over what others think, say and do. We want something or someone so badly that we will try to control as much of the situation as possible not realizing we are not the pilot of the plane. The position is pretty much the passenger...the backseat passenger at that. When you are a passenger, you have no control of the brakes. You are just riding. When reality finally hits, we decide to be the pilot and take control. There are feelings involved and that is always hard to deal with. The reality is YOU finally realize YOU deserve better and should not have gotten yourself in a situation where you KNEW or felt it was wrong, but you allowed your heart to interfere. You really love this person, but you ask yourself "do I love me more." No one wants to get hurt either way. You continue praying about the situation by asking God to remove it or make a way for things to work out. We have to be careful what we pray for.

Love is an addiction, and it is hard to break free from it. Love will have you doing things you know it is not right and it will also have you doing things that make sense. We cannot lose ourselves when loving someone or people because sometimes it is hard to find ourselves again. We cannot waste time waiting for someone to get their life together or finances paid off or get over the fear of what the other person will do. We have to be prepared for whatever the outcome will be. We have to be careful about the choices we make. We cannot always have what we want, but we will always have what we need. It is always hard when it comes to matters of the heart. Your brain and heart do not always agree and sometimes this is the reason it becomes difficult to make decisions. We

Keeping It Real

sometimes leave our brains outside and drag our hearts in with us. Most of the time it probably should be the other way around. We let our emotions control what we do. Our choices decide the consequences. If you choose to do something you know it is not spiritually or morally right, you will suffer the consequences. Sometimes it takes more than one person to tell someone to think about his or her spiritual life. We have to obey in order to be blessed.

We are all imperfect and face temptation probably every day, but we have choices. Also, do not allow that one you cannot have make you get out of character over something you know yourself is not worth it. For example, you know this person is legally bound, married, attached whatever, there is no reason to get angry when you can't go with him or her out of town, no reason to get mad because you can't be around her kids and/or family, no reason to get upset because you can't see him like you want to, absolutely NO reason to get pissed off because he or she can't or won't do anything for you, yet, don't mind having sex. DON'T beg anyone or keep talking to you are blue in the face for the simple things or to get him or her to do things for you. It causes frustration and stress between the both of you and truth be told THAT PERSON DOES NOT BELONG TO YOU no matter what reason(s) you are given. If you want to be real about it, you are single and will remain single until that person is DIVORCED. So, wanting what or who we can't have can cause misery, depression, loneliness, and stress. A question or two for you to think about. Can a married person have a girlfriend or boyfriend? Can a single person date a married person? Everyone has their own opinion regarding those two questions. Some will say "yes" and others will disagree. The fact of the matter is if a married person is dating a single person which is usually a side piece, girlfriend, or boyfriend, it's all a LIE. The

Keeping It Real

relationship   or   affair   is   not   true.

Keeping It Real

Authenticity

I named this chapter authenticity because a lot of times when you meet someone or begin a relationship it is a smokescreen. What I mean is some people will portray as someone else to get what they want. For instance, let us say a woman sends a text to her ex-lover stating she misses him, thinks about him every day, and hopes to see him soon as well as rekindling the relationship. All of those WORDS SOUND thoughtful and heartfelt, right? They are heart-wrenching to be honest. So, the guy decides to give it another chance. Now, they have history and have been back and forth a couple of times. Quite naturally things started off good for the two or three months until he started seeing the "true" person, the "real" or "authentic" person. All the "I love you" and "I appreciate you" began to diminish. He felt that he was the one saying those words more than she was. She started to act like everything he did or said bothered her. He is at the point where he is miserable and feels stuck. He even had to constantly ASK for a kiss. It had come to the point where all they did was the smack on the lip thing. The passionate kissing had ceased because of whatever excuses she came up with. He did not ask for much and it seemed there had to be a reason such as she be "in the mood" or if she had a good day. He also had to ask for sex. This made him mad because in the beginning it was not a problem for her. My point is that some people play the role

Keeping It Real

of another character in order to get what they really want. The same goes for creating friendships. It is all good at first, but you quickly see how that new friend or love changes. It is sad because it really doesn't take long to see how a person really is.

We have to be mindful of others and not allow ourselves to get used or taken advantage of. Our hearts feel, but our minds reveal. Our minds tell us to walk away and move on with our lives. Our hearts tell us to stay and see how things go. Then it's like a tug-of-war with the mind and heart. It is important to show who we really are from the beginning until the end. Once we see that we are being used, it can cause anger, resentment, and revenge. If we are not true to ourselves, how can we be true to anyone else? We are not perfect, but we need to be honest and transparent. I am sure you can relate in some way. How did you handle the situation or are you still dealing with it?

Have you heard of a narcissist? A narcissist is "an extremely self-centered person who has an exaggerated sense of self-importance" (Merriam-Webster, 2019). There are so many traits of a narcissist it is not even funny. I bet we all have at least one of those traits. A narcissist is one selfish ass person! Narcissists manipulate people, they think of themselves, say words they do not mean (literally), blame others for things they do, plays the victim role, are usually abandoned or wasn't shown love or how to love, will break up with their significant others or end their marriages before their partners do, and love to do things for others just to get notification. It is probably more to where that came from, but I've named enough. If you have ever been in a relationship with a narcissist or been around one, you can relate to what is mentioned above. A narcissist will make you go insane because you wreck your mind trying to

Keeping It Real

figure out what the hell YOU did wrong. You are the blame for EVERY damn thing that goes wrong. You can approach these types of people with the best intentions, such as a pleasant tone and carefully chosen words to prevent making them feel like you are blaming them, and it does not do a bit of good. Somehow, they will find a way to blame you regardless. Your intentions are so sincere, but narcissists do not perceive it that way. They feel you are attacking them which is guilty. Sometimes a narcissist will give gifts to make up for the guilt such as flowers or dinner. It does not matter because the next day it's the same mess. The situation is worse when you really love a narcissist. You will be taken advantage of in every way he or she can think of.

Narcissists not only exist in relationships, but it can be family members as well co-workers. The "on-the-job" narcissist is not accountable for anything and I mean that. That person never does anything wrong because someone else has to be blamed. He or she will take credit for work that he or she did not do. The family narcissists do the same thing. We have to break away from people like that because they will make you come out of character when you are trying to defend yourself. I asked if you have dealt with narcissists before because they are not real. They do not portray their true selves…in the beginning that it is. They only want a supply and if you do anything and I mean anything they do not like or feel you are hurting them they will leave you alone with the quickness. They will not have all of the facts. They just KNOW you are out to hurt them. Once you distance yourself from a narcissist, whether it is at work or a partner, do all you can to stay away from that person. As time goes by and you have not contacted him or her, you will be contacted. If you want to know more about narcissists, just do a Google search or check out a book at the

Keeping It Real

library. I guarantee you will be able to relate to everything you read.

Keeping It Real

Second Place

Let me us see! Where do I begin? Well, I am sure you are wondering what I mean by second place. There are a couple of things this title pertains to. In this case, it is a position in your relationship. Yes, I have mentioned relationships in many of the chapters. Our lives are surrounded by relationships whether it's with God, at work, or with another human being. We have to KNOW where we stand in people's lives particularly someone you love. When you are involved with someone who is married or in a relationship with someone else, you automatically place yourself in second place. No matter how much you love that person, you will still be second place. And no matter how much that person tells you that you are number one in his or her life, you are STILL second place. Truthfully, you are filling a void. The void where the spouse supposedly isn't doing his or her marital duties such as intimacy. No one what that person tells you…you ARE filling a void. You are doing what the other won't do. You may still miss out on holidays and other special occasions. And you may not miss out on holidays. It could be the type of situation where it just works out that you are able to be around that person's family including the kids if there are any. A lot of times you will not be able to be around the kids or go out in public with them because the kids are not supposed to know about you. There are some people who get as much attention as

Keeping It Real

the "main" chic or man.

Most of the time you are always alone, on standby, or waiting. The object of this game is WAITING. You wait for a phone call which is usually when he or she is at work, driving, or not around the family and/or spouse or significant other. If he or she does call you while at home, that person is most likely outside talking to you. If not, believe me, the conversation will be short, you will be carrying the conversation, and/or his or her answers will consist of one or two words. For example, "yes", "no", or "uh huh." You will see the patterns as time goes by. If you are an impatient person, do NOT put yourself on the back burner. Oh, I forgot to mention you will have to get a hotel room for privacy unless that person does not live with anyone. Even if that is the case, you will only be there for a limited amount of time or during a certain time of day or night which means the other person is at work, out of town, or wherever. Your holidays will be spent without the love of your life majority of the time because you are not number one. You are number two or three or four. Who knows? It can be depressing because you put your life on hold because you were told the marriage or relationship will be over or empty promises.

A person's actions always show the truth. If you are getting told to "bear with me" or "be patient" and nothing has changed except more "stuff" keeps coming up, you may want to consider walking away, but that's all up to you. People say if something is worth waiting for, it will not come easy. It can turn into months or even years before you are able to truly become number one. As I have mentioned above, "stuff" always comes up. The thing you have to realize is that YOU are in control! You may think that you are not in control, but you hold all of the cards. No one is being held against his or her own will to stay in that position. It is like a game of chess… you choose what position you want to play. On the

Keeping It Real

other hand, there are some people who do not mind being second at all. Why? It is because they are free to do what they want including dating other people. They can date whomever they want and no one to answer to. When you are in second place, a lot of times you do not know when you will see that person again. It's whenever he or she has time for you. On the outside looking in, you ARE in second place. You also have to think about getting caught. So, there are a lot of things to think about and you may always have to look over your shoulder. If her husband finds out she is having an affair, he can sue you for alienation of affection. It is not guaranteed he will win because there must be proof. We are given choices when it comes to allowing others in our lives.

All our choices have consequences whether they are good or bad. We have to figure out how valuable our time is and if the one you love is worth taking that valuable time. You love who you love and cannot help it. We must get our hearts and minds to be on one accord. A lot of times when it comes to love, it is very hard to do. If you have heard of the saying "love is blind", believe it! We see what we want to see and hear what we want to hear. We are on this earth to love one another, but sometimes love costs. Why do we always do ourselves wrong? Its no sense in waiting for someone to get his or her shit together. Why should you wait for any man or woman to leave the marriage or relationship for YOU? Will he or she every do it? You could have been married or at least engaged to someone else, yet, you chose to be second. You chose to give away your freedom to someone who could possibly be lying about leaving. Let us be real for a moment. IF the relationship or marriage is that bad then why is that person still there? You keep hearing the same excuse over and over. You have even offered a place to stay to start the separation process if the person is married. You really have no business screwing with someone who is tied to someone else anyway. So, why do we do

Keeping It Real

it? We do it because we believe what we are told. We believe they are really leaving until they prove otherwise. You will never be the one to be called in case there is an emergency. Never! You can live five minutes away and not get a call until AFTER he or she gets home. You may get invited to the hospital, but, believe you me, no one else will be there. You are an afterthought basically. As far as meeting other family members such as aunties and uncles and cousins, it won't happen unless they know about you and even then, you still won't be around them. And funerals and family reunions are out of the picture! You will not be riding in the family limo or out of town for her family functions. None of the things you long for or are used to doing in a relationship will happen UNLESS your Boo does not care! Sometimes they do not care who finds out or who knows but really it depends on WHO knows.

One important question to ask yourself is if he or she was asked if an affair were going on, would that person admit it? It is important because it will really shed light on where you really stand. He may tell you that he would not lie if his SO or wife asked him. Would you believe it? If she had to go to court because of the divorce, would she lie on the stand? You will not know unless you are physically in the courtroom. The problem is people "say" a lot of things. Words do not mean anything without actions. This is a situation we should not get ourselves into. We do because of our hearts and giving chances that hardly ever or never come into fruition. We gamble with our lives every day and it gets more dangerous when we involve "unattached" people. We are always wondering what that person is doing. Are they having sex with him or her? Are they at the mall or grocery store with the family? Are they cuddled on the couch watching a movie? Where are you? You are at home ALONE about to go off because you are thinking and overthinking. You check social media pages often and every day to

Keeping It Real

see if there are any pics. You look for minor details such as an arm around the waist or hand holding or even a kiss. You look for stuff that will make you break it off in a split second without feeling any guilt for doing it. Guess what? You do not find anything. Why? It could be because you WANT to find something because you are depressed, miserable, lonely, and angry. You have put up with bull crap you know deep down you should not have, but you believe all of the excuses. The bottom line is control…get some!

You can walk away and swear not to look back, but those heart strings reel you right back in. For what though? You want to find out if things will change or you do not want anyone else to have that person. You are afraid if you walk away for good, he or she will find someone else after divorcing or breaking up. You think about all those months even years of your life given away or wasted will be given to someone else. The reality is you were never his or hers in the beginning. Let them tell it and it would not be true. They will swear out your relationship IS real. It is real to him or her because of the love each other. You may be questioned if you feel he is worth the wait. You know, that reverse psychology stuff. "If you feel I'm worth it then you will wait." Oh and the "please be patient" or "please bear with me a little while longer" gets old. What do you do? You wait a little while longer because you do not want to prove her wrong. You have given yourself limits such as 6 months or maybe even a year. Yet, things continue to "come up." Where do you stand? You are in the exact same spot because you chose not to move your chess piece. You chose to see what exactly is keeping that person home. What is it?!!!! What is it?!!!! What?!!! You know who it is? It is not the other person. It is YOU! You are holding YOU back. You do not want to find out "if it's meant to be it will be." You do not want to hear that mess because you want IT to be NOW…right now. You know its true, but you have been waiting a long time. We turn blind eyes and deafen our ears to situations we know we should not be in. We have to do better because no one can judge us but the Man above. We have our own account with Him. I know a large part of this book discusses relationships, but that is what people are. We RELATE to one another in some way. The point is DO **NOT** WAIT FOR NO MAN OR WOMAN TO LEAVE HIS OR HER WIFE OR HUSBAND, GIRLFRIEND OR BOYFRIEND! **DO NOT DO IT!** You can choose to wait if you want to and feel it is best for YOU.

Keeping It Real

Everyone Ain't You

We have to really think about the things we do and say regarding others. It can sometimes take awhile to realize that everyone doesn't think like you. Everyone doesn't love like you. Everyone doesn't communicate the way you do. Everyone doesn't treat people the same way you do. Everyone doesn't put up with the same things you tolerate. Everyone doesn't like the same things you like or dislike. Everyone doesn't have the same work ethics you portray. Everyone doesn't clean or cook the way you do. Everyone perceives things differently. I'm sure you get the point. Everyone is different and we have to think about that more often than we probably want to.

An opportunity can be presented to two people and it's possible their choices can be totally opposite. You may tolerate certain things in a relationship whereas another person would not tolerate the same things. Everyone ain't you! We all deal with situations differently. You may be the type of person who keep in touch with your friends and family members. Others may not communicate as much with their loved ones. You have to remember just because you do it doesn't mean other people will. We have to learn how to separate ourselves from this frame of mind because it may cause you to dissociate yourself, worry, and try to

Keeping It Real

control something you have no control over. It's sometimes hard not to think about or worry about the things we can't control. We sometimes want to fix everything, every problem, and everyone. We know we do not have the capability to fix everything...ONLY God can do that. There are ones who are givers, takers, watchers, talkers and doers. You have to figure out what type of person you are and learn how to compromise and deal with the people who do things totally opposite because EVERYONE AIN'T YOU. If everyone thought the same and did the same things, I guess the world would be boring. I don't know, maybe not. A difference of opinion isn't always a bad thing and sometimes it's not always good either. When it comes to raising our children, we see how they react to situations and how they talk. A lot of times you will see yourself in your children. For instance, the generation now is a whole lot different than 25-30 years ago. There is a lot of technology such as the internet, advanced video games, and smartphones. In the 90s there was no internet nor smartphones. The video games were not as advanced and animated as they are today. The younger generation tend to stay inside to play video games or spend more time using their cellular phones. The older ones spent more time outside to play with friends until it got dark or before the street light came on. This just shows how people and things have changed over the years. We have learned to adapt and keep it moving. We have to do that as we see the differences in others and always remember...everyone ain't you.

Keeping It Real

Misunderstood

Do you ever feel like people do not ever understand what you say? They do not "get you" or comprehend when you express your feelings or even explaining something. And you may think "what the heck is it that you are not understanding." You have to learn that everyone does NOT perceive the same way you do. It can be annoying at times but it's also amazing in a sense because that's how the Creator made us. If everyone was the same, who knows how this world would be. A lot of times it's hard to get people to understand how we feel, what we say, and what we do. For example, expressing how you feel about someone, or something can be difficult because the other person may not actually "hear" what you are saying. You can tell someone you want to be friends first and allow that friendship to turn into a relationship, but it doesn't mean he or she understands. A child may try to explain that he is upset about something that happened, but it just isn't coming out right on "your" end. We have to have patience, understanding and empathy when listening to others.

Oftentimes, what we say is not what other people hear. Sometimes you have to break stuff down for others so they can understand or put your words in layman's terms. A lot of times you get tired of feeling misunderstood, so you are

Keeping It Real

tired of explaining how you feel or what you mean all of the time. You have to realize that everyone will not understand you and that's okay. Everyone is not on the same level as you. Sometimes people may think you are argumentative because you keep it real and opinionated. You have a strong personality and it's not always a bad thing. You just have to remember that everyone is NOT on YOUR level. A lot of times you probably don't mean to hurt anyone's feelings and sometimes you may think "oh yeah I meant exactly what I said so get over it." Because everyone is so different, you won't be able to please everyone and honestly there are probably a select few of people you really want to please…on this earth that is. The number one person is God. For we misunderstood people, try praying for the right words to say but still get your point across as well getting that person to understand you.

Keeping It Real

Faces of a Mistress

I know when people see the word mistress they think of a man or woman cheating on the spouse. Yes, that's one mistress but a mistress doesn't have to be the "homewrecker" as people call it. A mistress can also be a habit that someone has such as smoking or gambling. We can talk about the obvious...the extramarital affair. It doesn't matter what the "situation" is at that person's home it's still an affair. If she tells you that she and her husband are divorcing, watch what she does. Does she make arrangements to move out and get her own place or move in with a family member? Does she sleep in a separate room until she sees her way out financially...whenever that is? He tells you that he had plans to leave the marriage BEFORE you came into the picture but so much time has gone by and he's still there. Either way the both of you have a choice to make. You can stick around and see what he does or continue seeing other people until you see otherwise. The "outsider" is not obligated to wait for him or her to leave. Sometimes we make the choice to give that person the benefit of a doubt because we want to see how things go. But there comes a time when you get tired of waiting. Time does not wait for anyone and putting your life on hold just to see how things go will only last but so long.

Keeping It Real

Love has a way of making us blind to reality. The heart and the brain do not always agree because the heart is full of emotions. The brain is logical and tells you to be sensible but there goes that heart again. The thing about being the "third" party is majority of the time you are alone. While she is out with the family…the whole family, you are at home alone or maybe you are spending time with your family or friends. Can he post a picture of you on social media just to let you shine for a little bit? Remember that YOU CAN do a lot of things that he or she CAN'T because of the legality of being married to someone else. When you get together is it night or during the day? Most of the time you are spending time at night and almost always talking on the phone while that person is working. You have to decide what's best for you and also think about what if you get caught or the spouse finds out. In some states the spouse can sue for alienation of affection and a lot of the cases win. Besides, all of the time you spend waiting for him or her to leave or whatever, that time could be spent with someone who is SINGLE and have time for you. What are you going to do? Let's move on to something else. When people gamble it can be just for fun but there are times where it becomes repetitive. It can become an addiction which can lead to lying and stealing. For example, when it becomes an addiction, he or she will lie about where they have been or who they have been with.

Keeping It Real

Personal Thoughts

The purpose of this chapter is to get perspectives from across the board. I wanted to know how a female and male feel regarding the questions below. These are opinions of both males and females, young and old.

How do you feel about someone mistreating you in ways such as being disrespectful and taking advantage of your kindness? "I feel used, upset, and hurt by that individual sometimes so much that I tend to lash out and/or shut down completely on others. Many times I wonder why me and why now, what I did to deserve this." (38-year-old, female) "That's a no, no. First, I know that I am somebody, not a child. I respect myself and I sure do expect the same from someone else. If you let someone mistreat you, your kindness is being taken advantage of. You are making me feel if I'm nothing." (57-year-old male) "When you are treated badly, disrespected, and taken advantage of, it can destroy your self-esteem and sometimes your whole being. You must not allow that, man or woman. Someone treating you badly cannot truly really have your best interest. People sometimes become conditioned to abuse and accept it, please don't." (61-year-old female) "I will feel hurt and angry because that person has gave it they're all to the point of not loving again. He/she took in the values of their time and energy plus patience to be kind and generous to find out that it no longer existed in the other person's mind. (34-year-old male)

Do you feel some men or women prefer to be with someone who mistreats them rather than be with someone who treats them well? This is based on society today. "In my opinion, men and women want to be with someone who treats them well, however, many have showed that they don't care as long as they have companionship." (38-year-old, female) "Even in today's society what man or woman wants to be with a person who mistreats them? To me, being mistreated is just like saying you belong to me. I can treat you any way I like. I can say anything or I can do anything and it will be okay. That is not the way it's supposed to be. Treat me the way I deserve to be treated. Show me the love and affection I deserve and I'll show you the same." (57-year-old male) "I believe that to be true. Someone who prefers that way must be convinced he or she deserved no less, and should do some soul searching and look within yourself. I think it goes back to self-esteem. Love yourself." (61-year-old female) Yes and no. The yes part is when they grow up in a household that is run by their parents they take notice of the daily situations that go on in the house and they will adapt to thinking its ok like the cussing, fighting, divorce, who keeps the kids etc. The No part is when they take a stand and talk to the person who is being mistreated saying "baby when you grow up this is not the situation to be involved in." (34-year-old male)

Do you feel we should condemn ourselves and/or others for things done in the past? "No, I don't feel that we should condemn others for their mistakes in the past. What's done in the past should stay there." (38-year-old, female) Í do not think no one should be condemned for their past if they have made peace with themselves and with God. If you never let go of the past, how can you ever go on with the future. Make peace with yourself and God and move on." (57-year-old male) "No, we can't condemn anyone including ourselves. It is easier said than done. Learning to forgive comes from God. You can beat yourself up, but you got to go back to God. That is a difficult thing for some people to do. They may want to base forgiveness on what happened and how they were affected. However, you cannot hold grudges from the past and have a future. (61-year-old female) If I'm answering the question right, I think yes we should condemn ourselves that's done in the past because the mistakes we made should make us stronger and help us not to make the same mistakes in the past and to look further in the near future. (34-year-old male)

Do you think someone who has been hurt should punish others? "No, as I stated in number 3 what's done in the past should stay in the past, however, we as human beings we often do put blame on what others have done during their pasts." (Michelle-38-years-old) "No, trying to hurt someone else because you have been hurt is not the answer. Sometimes you got to think seriously 'what will I gain?' Hurting others mean you are just like the person who hurt you. Before you hurt someone else, the best thing is to move on. The person that hurt you will get hers or his one day." (James-57-years-old) "No, it's hard enough dealing with your issues. Repair your brokenness." (Linda-61-years-old) "No, the person that has been hurt should let the other person know what happened, that's if he/she feels comfortable discussing the situation. Because punishing can be in different forms, but don't give the person the satisfaction or upper hand because no one is perfect." (34-years-old male)

What does having a relationship with God, your husband or wife, significant other, children, and your parents mean to you? "I believe if you don't have God first then the other family members as well as yourself turmoil. Praying, communicating, trust, and love play a part in a household." (38-year-old, female) "Having a relationship with God and my wife means a lot because without God none of this is possible. I know that if He's with me no one can be against me" (57-year-old male) "Without my relationship with God, there is really no peace within, even if home and family seems to be good, you are really empty. It enables you to cope with life. That's why I say 'Oh well!' I have my Comforter." (Linda-61-years-old) "Having a relationship with God is incredible because he sees no wrong only right. If you pray and repent, he will relieve you from everything that you are going through whether it is good or bad. He will always be there where ever you are at. Having a relationship with a significant other is great too because it is the three of them, you, your significant, and God. What discussion that y'all have between each other God is listening praying and healing." (34-years-old male)

What is your life testimony? "My testimony is I thought I found my Boaz, my rib, at the age of 23 but 7-10 years later that I realized he wasn't, I was cheated on, I was disrespected, and emotionally scarred. I tried 3 times to make my marriage work, however, I learned you cannot keep something that doesn't want to be kept. As I get older I understand that he wasn't meant for me and I forgave him 2 years ago but I still haven't found that special one. I love hard and I'm a challenge because my past hinders my future because I remember how I was done wrong and I'm afraid to trust or to fall in love again." (Michelle-38-years-old) "First, treat everyone the way you want to be treated. Love everyone even sometimes you do not want to do it. Second, when you are in a relationship, make sure that the feelings are mutual. As I always say, loving someone is different from being in love. My reason for that is you can love anyone and be okay with them. When you are in love, you know that this is someone you can give your all and all and this is the right someone." (57-years-old male)

"I am 61 years of age and still not sure of my testimony, but I want to be a valuable, educated, intellectual and spiritual person. I want to be able to impart some wisdom to my grandchildren hoping they will listen. I believe the longer you live, you should use your time wisely. You can accomplish a lot with God's blessing." (Linda - 61-years-old) "My life testimony is to surround myself with positive people who want to have something that will benefit me in the long run. I have two sisters that I love and adore so much and I want to be just like them. One day I want to own a house, pay mortgage, and have a happy life. I want to be stress-free and get closer to God and to live eternity in heaven, wash away my sins, remove hurt, hatred, whatever is in my heart away, and remove this sadness that I feel going through everyday struggle. I want my mother, (and tell my father), brothers, and sisters to say "I am so proud of you I really am I know you can do it, see you have potential and you can put your mind to it." My brother and mom are saying you need to do this and that. I want to show the world that it is hope if you in jail or going through something. It is a second, third, and fourth chance. I am going to make a change. I am going to make a difference. I am going to pursue my career if it is the last thing I do. One day I am going to change a person(s) life and turn it around not just so I can feel good but to let them see they can do it just believe in God and themselves. This is my testimony." (34-years-old male)

Keeping It Real

POEMS by Karlie

Unhealed Wounds
The past hurt and pain was too much to bear
How do you move forward to be happy again
It starts with loving yourself
Until you never shed another tear.
The wounds do not seem to want to heal
Because you are always thinking "why me"
Pray for peace of mind
To stop worrying about back then.
To find true happiness you must forgive
Or the wounds will never heal
Because all you really need is to do God's Will.

Beauty Marks
The marks left from last night
Thinking of how good things were
At that moment it felt good, it felt right
Beauty marks of the night
Oh but these marks aren't like tattoos
They slowly fade away until they are gone
As they fade you think of how quickly they appeared
The night before is only a blur
Filled with whispers in the ear
These beauty marks represent passion of the past
They slowly disappear because they are not meant to last

Keeping It Real

Confident Man
Your wit and intelligence brightens up any day
The way you talk about life uplifts spirits abound
Your dimpled smile shines like a star
You are tough but gentle
You are one of a kind
A confident man is someone like you
Your drive to live life is so liberating
You are independent and strong yet caring too
Continue being the great and confident man you were made to be.

Never Forget Me and You
I am the woman who will pray for you
I am the woman who has your back
When you are burdened with life's troubles
I am the one who will uplift you.
You are the man I want to be with
Someone to share my hopes and dreams
Your heart is very fragile and very hard to mend
Let me be the one who treats you like a king.
I know you are worthy of having a woman like me
Because I know I am worthy of having a man like you
Never forget who we have come to be
Never forget about you and me.

You Are a King
You are the provider, the worker, the master
You are a King
You are the man that people look up to
You are a King
You were not created to be without a queen
You are a king
You are tough yet gentle and kind
Set your heart free from hurt and pain
Set your heart free so you can live again
You deserve to be happy just give it a chance
Never forget that you are a King

Keeping It Real

Changing Faces
Please do not act like I mean something today
Then pretend I do not exist the very next day
Your needs have been met
So I'm no use to you
Your face has changed
Now there are two of you

Powerless
The many thoughts of a painful past
Has taken over your life
You ask why does this happen to me
Why so much strife
Your power has been stripped away
You struggle to get it back
You need relief to move on but do not know where to go
First things first get on your knees and ask Him to lead the way
Get your power back to live your life again

When It is Good
It is good to you when it makes you feel special
It is good for you when you are pain-free
Respectful, caring, gentle and kind is how it should be
Your life seems filled with joy it is hard to believe
When it is good you have more pep in your step
The good outweighs the bad when things are great
You are finally able to feel the love you've hoped for
Someone in your life who you can adore
If it is good hold on to it
Do not risk losing what you deserve
Because if you do you may not get it back
So cherish and love what you have

Keeping It Real

From the Outside
From the outside looking in, there is a different picture
The outside tells a story that you cannot see
Put yourself in someone else's shoes to visualize the scene
As you look through the lenses of the person you face
Maybe you will be able to change your ways
From the outside looking in it is not always what it seems
From the outside looking in there is sometimes fear
Because what you may be thinking and what you actually see is usually the truth
So pay attention to the words you say and the things you do
Because the person on the outside is looking at you

Slow Burn
The calls were often and many
Messages flowed each day like waves in the ocean
There were several date nights each week
After a while the calls become short chats
Each conversation struggles to stay afloat
You no longer have many words to say
The candle that was shining so brightly starts to dim
The slow burn is what it is called
Until the candle flickers no more

I Do not Trust You
You say what you will do
But you never do what you say
You want me to trust you
Yet it's not easy for me to believe what's true
So why should I trust you
We are supposed to be honest in everything that we say and do
It seems your words hold no meaning
Unless you show and prove
Seeing is believing and that's the truth
Since I don't see anything
I can't trust you

Keeping It Real

Pretending
Your heart will not let you see
What's in front of your face
Because your mind is running a different race
You know that what you see is true
But your heart won't agree with you
So you pretend that things are not what they are really are
The thoughts you have are just delusions thus far
So you go through life pretending that things are real
Because in reality you don't know how to feel

I Am Not A Doormat
You tell me you like me and love me
Just to keep me around
Your lips speak such sweet lies
Until you need something from me
Once you get what you want
You wipe your feet all over me
I am not a doormat
I am loyal to you because you are mine
I expect the same from you
Not sporadically but all of the time
You get royal treatment just like a king
You know the inner workings of my mind
You plan your next move to get what you want
I give in and get hooked just like you thought
I am not a doormat
I am not something to wipe your dirty feet on
I have a heart made of gold
With beauty that shows from inside out
I'm fragile just like glass
So you must handle with care
I am not a doormat so don't take it there

Keeping It Real

Kicking Me When I'm Down
I'm going through a lot as you can see
Why talk ugly and down to me
My life is stressed and strained to the max
The last thing I need is more pain
Instead of kicking me while I'm low
Uplift me in prayer
We are to love our brothers and sisters no matter what
God says to treat one another with care
In order to be blessed, we must not fail
So stop pressing me down
I'm begging you please
Stop kicking me when I'm down
I'm already on my knees

The Makings of You
I don't think I've ever met anyone like you
No, as a matter of fact, I've never met anyone like you
I've known of you for 20 years
But I've never met anyone like you
Your gentle and caring demeanor
Is comforting as a warm blanket on a cold day
You see the beauty of this caramel brown queen
And you're not afraid to show it
These are the makings of you
Kind yet strong, loving but brave
Handsome, clean-shaven and mmm smell good too
You see this man is definitely different from the others
He knows a woman's worth and I'm not talking about between the sheets
He came at the right time
It was meant for us to meet
God will remove the one who keeps you down
And replaces them with who you need
So if there is someone in your life who treats you like a king or queen
My advice is keep them close and see what life brings

Keeping It Real

Drowning
I cannot swim
I cannot swim
Life's anxieties are weighing me down
To the point where I am choking
It seems I have no choice but to drown
I cannot swim
I can only take baby steps
In this deep shallow body of water
It seems the more steps I take
The longer the wait
I cannot swim
I reach out for those who I help
Just to get turned away
The same people who come to me when needed
But are not there for me
I'm still drowning
Some days I'm low and some I'm high
And other days I question why
One thing is for sure I do call on God
Because through all of my mess
He is the one who has answers to all of my tests
I raise my hand through the heavy waves
In hopes of someone coming to save me
I scream out in agony
Will anyone see me
I feel a tug then a pull
Thank God I'm free

Degradation
Sticks and stones may break my bones but words will never hurt me
Who made up this tale
Anyone who has a spine or something bigger – a heart - will feel hurt and pain
Sometimes the words someone says can make you go insane
You have been called a low life, bastard, scum, dead beat
A bitch, a whore, or even a trick

Keeping It Real

I think I would rather be hit with a stick
Because I can pick up something and defend myself
Words hurt more than a fist to the face or chest
They burn like fire to wood
His words are like black eyes
Sore and swollen at first
After the swelling goes down there is this dark spot
Consisting of remnants of her degrading words
How you wish you can forget
About everything your ears heard
Just when you think you have finally healed from the words of the sword
Here it comes again
Degradation is something you can't seem to avoid

30 Year Love

It's been almost 30 years since I last saw you
All I remember is how you were crushing on me
You were a mannish little boy
But it was always fun having you around
Little did I know your feelings were deep for me until now
After all of this time you still feel the same
Even though you have made a family for yourself and gave someone else your name
I've been where you are but now things have changed
Why can't our situations be the same
Talking to you and seeing you have brought up feelings I never knew I had
I was told it's never too late to find "The One"
But how easy do you think that is
When we are not on the same page
I wonder if there will be a chance for us in this lifetime
Because now that we have grown up I definitely don't mind
Things are going the way we want them to at this moment
But how long will it last
You said that if you ever saw me again and had the change to be with me you would take it
Here I am willing and able to see what I've missed
I guess the only thing left to do is be patient

Keeping It Real

The Other Woman
She is the side piece who does what the other one won't
She is sometimes the well-kept secret
And sometimes there is no disguise
You ask who "she" is huh
She is the mistress, the other woman
She falls in love with him as if he's her man
Just to get disappointed again and again
Promises of having a future with her
Sayings from his lying lips sound so sweet to the ear
But in reality she hears what she wants to hear
She asks herself why did she put herself in this love affair
Knowing that nothing is really there
She asks him if it's just lust
And he quickly says no without hesitation
Yet deep down she still feels what he says isn't true
She's his baby his sweetheart but is she really
Will they be together
She wonders will he leave
No one really knows but him and God
She's scared because she's already given away her heart
With hopes it doesn't get torn apart
The other woman is a homewrecker is what people say
But do they understand its two ways
Will she wait for this unavailable man to rescue her
From all of her doubts and fears
Will he make her wait for days, months or years
She has control over this affair but she doesn't want to let him go
She wonders why, why, why has she done this to herself
Her heart won't agree with her brain
Even though it's really quite simple and she knows
The other woman is who she is and that's the way it goes

Keeping It Real

Second to None (The Other Woman Part 2)
As time goes by she realizes there is no time for her
Always alone and standing by for calls, text messages, visits too
If it's not on her time then what can she do
She makes it her business to make room for him
Later realizing it really doesn't matter
Because she can't see him when she wants to
This feeling she gets keeps getting worse
She asks herself why does she deal with it
Not thinking she made the choice a long time ago
Even though she made a promise to herself never to do that again
She knows deep down she's settling
But her heart says no
She tries convincing herself that it ain't so
Sticking by this man that ain't even hers
Still waiting and waiting until he's free
Often thinking how stupid can she be
The "runner up" is all she is
She's not first but last on the list
No matter how many times she's told
To stick by him until she's able to have and to hold
But the day will come when she finally sees
How she will not continue to be second or even last
The day when she will keep looking ahead
She will not take anything less than being first
Because this beautiful black Queen will be second to none

When a Man Is Hurt
He feels his heart has been broken into a million pieces
And he doesn't know what to do
So he decides to stop caring
About everything and everyone
He beats himself up even though he's not the blame
He wonders if he can get passed the shame
That he feels because things will never be the same
When a man is hurt he builds a wall

Keeping It Real

So no other woman can come in
The pride he has no longer exists
His heart is broken and will be hard to heal
He hides his sorrow until he becomes distant and cold
When a man hurts he doesn't cry out for help
He decides he can handle it alone
But he cries in silence where no one can see
How much his heartache has taken over him
He wonders how much longer he can take the pain
He wonders if things will ever be the same
Will he ever let anyone back in
Will he ever fall in love again
Only he will know when that time comes
When a man is hurt he doesn't tell a soul
He hides behind a mask by day
And by night he looks a totally different way
To the man that is hurting this too shall pass
The pain in your heart is only temporary
The achiness inside will soon disappear
Just have faith this will not last

You Don't Care
When I reach out to you about how I feel
It doesn't seem to concern you
If what you hear doesn't apply to you
Then you turn a deaf ear
My feelings are just as important as yours
I am not exempt from any pain or sorrow
You don't care for the words I say
If you did you would find a way
To show you are there for me as much as I am there for you
Sometimes I don't know what to do
Is it even worth pouring my heart out to you
I guess that's a decision I will need to carefully make
I can't force you to respond or reply
But what I do know is I refuse to ask why
Because it's clear you don't care

Keeping It Real

Or maybe you don't know what to say
I can't read your mind or make you say a word
If how I feel really matters then lend me your listening ear
Otherwise it's a waste of time
And we will continue to stay here

Diamond in the Rough
She wonders if she will ever be good enough
Will she be pretty enough
Someone like her comes a dime a dozen
But deep down she doesn't really know
Sometimes she doesn't feel she's worth it
Others say she is beautiful
But she doesn't think so
She doesn't see how shiny she is among all of the chipped and broken jewels
This woman stands out from all of the rest
But to everyone who knows her, she's really one of the best
She looks in the mirror not liking the reflection
Yet she still smiles
As she looks in the mirror she wants to know
What everyone else sees
Saying to herself "they can't be talking about me"
She's a straight Diamond in the Rough
She learns to walk with confidence and strength
Even though sometimes she gets weak
It's God who she continues to seek
Who is 'she' you may ask
This is a beautiful, rare trinket that is hard to find
She's in the midst of a mine full of gold that can never ever be sold
She is made of many colors and has a unique shape too
Who is this Woman, this Lady, this Queen
She is a Mother, a Friend, a Provider
She's caring, she's smart, she's tough
But among all of these things she's
A Diamond in the Rough

Keeping It Real

Free Yourself
You are constantly reminded of how things used to be
Your heart is filled with so much love
You know deep down things aren't right
Yet you yearn so much to be set free
Free yourself from the deep pain inside
Make it go away you beg and plead
Make it go away because you're in dire need
Every day you think about why things happen the way they do
Your choices haven't been the best
You know this to be true
You feel like flying away just like a bird
The weight of your past is holding you down
It seems to always appear in your present
Because there is a void to be filled
Forgive the ones who have hurt you
So you can move on
Forgive yourself for the things you've done
Free yourself, free yourself, free yourself

Sometimes I Get Sad
There are days when I'm blue
There are days when I'm happy
And there are days when I just don't know what to do
There is loneliness, bitterness and anger within
How do I manage to get through this pain
How do I get back to normal again
Or were things really normal in the beginning
Sometimes my thoughts make me sad
And at times they make me mad
Will my life ever take a turn
Down the road to peace and joy
I know praying to God is the only way
To remove these feelings I have
Because He is the ruler over all things
So this too shall pass

Keeping It Real

You Don't Care
When I reach out to you about how I feel
It doesn't seem to concern you
If what you hear doesn't apply to you
Then you turn a deaf ear
My feelings are just as important as yours
I am not exempt from any pain or sorrow
You don't care for the words I say
If you did you would find a way
To show you are there for me as much as I've been there for you
Sometimes I don't know what to do
Is it even worth pouring my heart out to you
I guess that's a decision I will need to carefully make
I can't force you to respond or reply
But what I do know is I refuse to ask why
Because it's clear you don't care
Or maybe you don't know what to say
I can't read your mind or make you say a word
If how I feel really matters
Then lend me your listening ear
Otherwise it's a waste of time
And we will remain here

Nobody's Here
Opening the door to hear no sound
You yell "I'm home!" but no one is around
There are countless nights with no one there
No one to talk to and nothing to share
Loneliness sets in each and every night
You constantly think "why am I always alone?"
Nobody is here no one is home
How you hope there are open arms
To hug you tight when you get home
Nobody's here you say but that can change

Keeping It Real

As long as you have family
You will never be alone
As long as you have God
You will see how happy you can be
There will be a day when you're not alone
And no more saying "anyone here?"
So continue praying for what you want
And see what God has to bring

Waiting for a Lifetime
Waiting and wanting
Wanting and waiting
For the love of your life to come
Waiting for that special person to break free
Your patience is wearing thin because you don't know when
The time will come to love completely again
She's with someone else this you do know
He's still with her but just can't seem to let go
You wait for calls you wait for dates
You wonder will it be too late
For the love you have inside your heart
To be dispersed like stars in the sky
You are limited and tied where there's little room to move
It seems it's never on your time it's always "see you soon"
Waiting for a lifetime is what it seems
A lifetime of seconds, minutes, hours, and days
Time that is wasted away
Asking yourself if this is worth the wait
You can never get back the time invested in others
But you do have a choice one way or another
To wait for your blessing or push it away
What God has for you is for you
Because that's the only way

Keeping It Real

Longing for You
Wondering when will the day come
For you to be mine for good
The waiting and waiting is a lot to deal with each day
When you love and long for someone you can't have does not help in any way
I love you and want you
What more can I say
Time is not on my side and it's true
This waiting and longing and longing and waiting
I don't know what to do
I'm giving it to God as you told me to
But why should my love be hidden from the world
Because someone else doesn't want a great person like you
Why should I conceal my face
When it seems I'm the one in first place
Love can be so blind at times
Longing for you and hoping for the best
Trying not to let the Devil steal my joy
It's hard when you long for someone so special
It's hard when you're looking through the window but can't go in
It's hard to keep all of this love tucked away
From the most important people in our lives
I long for you every second, every minute, every hour, every day
I know with time things will come into view
I will hold on as long as I can
Because I love and eagerly long for you

Careless
His feelings are a major concern for her
Because she loves him so much
And she craves his every touch
But the moment he shows a different side
She will start questioning what he may be trying to hide
The moment she stops doing the little things
Is the moment she begins her careless journey
The moment her words stop matching her actions

Keeping It Real

He will doubt everything she says
His actions will change just as hers
She will think he's being absurd
When he stops caring there is nothing she can do
Somewhere along the way he lost faith in her
When he stops caring her hands are tied
All of the things that used to matter no longer exist
And his beautiful smile he starts to hide
When she stops caring his efforts become futile
By that time it's too late
Her demeanor changes as he will see
Just how careless and callus she can be
So take my advice and pay attention to her
When he stops caring there's no turning back
She must hold onto him and keep her love intact

Hourglass
Both ends have beautiful sand
One end has more than the other
The more sand you have the more time you get
The less sand you see
The less time will be
You've waited more than 365 days
There's not much time left
The hourglass has been turned too many times already
Your life seems to be passing you by
It makes you wonder why continue to try
Life is too precious to waste
You continue to give your all
Just to keep being stalled
The hourglass is half full
What are you going to do now
Look at the reflection in the mirror
Do you like what you see
Go ahead and set yourself free
From the lonely nights and constant fear
You are worth more than you think

Keeping It Real

Don't allow the blessing waiting for you to sink
Time is moving fast
You hold on but how long will it last

Once a Week But Everyday
When will I see you again is the question always asked
Every day he hears her voice
She hears his every day too
Talking on the phone just isn't enough
So what are they going to do
They see each other once a week very seldom twice
And wish there could be more time
Because once a week just isn't nice
It has to be a better way of making room for her
Once a week but every day is all it seems to be
The reality is he has no availability
So what is left to do to fill this wedge
But constantly wait until the next time there is a date
If this relationship is going to last
There has to be a change
If this relationship is going to last
Things will remain the same
The less they see each other
The more anxious they get
They have to keep their hopes up and refuse to quit

Why Am I Here
Why am I here
Without no kids no husband no one at all
I come to an empty place
What to do with all of this space
Why am I here
All alone and oftentimes sad
It gets so lonely and boring
A lot of times I don't know what to do
Why am I here
In a city far away from my family

Keeping It Real

Whom I see only when I go home
There is an empty space in my heart
Why am I here
Is a question I ask myself
Was it the right choice or way to go
It must be because God is running the show
I'm here because I prayed and prayed for an answer
The doors were opened and I walked through
With hopes and trust things will work out
I'm learning when you ask God for anything there should be no doubt

Hidden No More
The day has come when I'm no longer a secret
I am a person with feelings
Or don't you see
You have to stop hiding me
From certain people you don't want to know
About the woman you've loved from so long ago
When you love someone you tell the world
Not tuck that person away
Until you are ready to reveal
Just how beautiful this woman is
I will not hide anymore and that's a fact
I am a diamond in the rough
So rare so unique
A precious stone that should not be part of hide and seek
Precious stones are out in the open
For everyone to see
I will no longer be on the side
Like trash on the street
I will be hidden no more
From the truth that's for sure
Open your eyes and look closely
As this queen walk right out of the door

Keeping It Real

You Are My Heart
You have a smile that is infectious and alluring
And a love that is breathtaking
You've got a hold on me that's for sure
That I don't know want to shake
You are my heart and that's no lie
A lot of times I ask why oh why
A man like you who is fit to be a king
You are one of the best things that's happened to me
Your love is so sweet and endearing as a forehead kiss
Thank you for asking God to bring me back to you
You have my heart so don't let it go
Cherish it, protect it, and handle it with care
Because the love I have inside of me is very rare
Despite the many obstacles that are in our way
My love for you gets stronger each day
The thought of you being thrown away
Constantly breaks my heart
My love for you is endless just like the oceans and seas
It would kill me inside if we're ever torn apart
When I think of you, I smile
Because nothing else seems to matter
When I'm away from you, it feels like a lifetime
When we're together, time won't stop flying
You are my heart and I pray it stays that way
I love you so much and that's something I never want to stop saying

They Don't Know
They don't know that he goes home alone every day
Do they know she yearns for love
Can they see that she struggles in every way
Can they sense she wants to scream
Because her life is not what it really seems
Do they know he's in love with someone he can't have
How she deals with the agony of waiting

Keeping It Real

For that person who he knows he will never get
They don't know she is no longer married
Or how he endures financial struggles
What they see is a smile that hides
All of the anxieties inside
Do they know she has envy sometimes
Because he can't buy the things they can
Is it written on her face the childhood pain
Or do they see that expression of glee
Who really is the fool…him or them
They don't know she is tired of life
And he constantly questions why
Must she always endure her trials
Over and over and over again
He wonders when will it ever end
Can they sense she cringes when they talk about their spouses
Because he no longer can relate
She tries to control the feeling of hate
Can they see she misses the feeling of someone waiting at home for her
They just don't know it's all a blur
Do they know it hurts him to smile
When he carries the weight of his troubles
She longs for someone to sweep her off of her feet
But the reality is there is no one
They just don't know he fakes it every day
Until she gets home and takes off her mask
Until the next day just to do it all over again
Do they really know how he feels
What they don't know is what's on the outside isn't real

Limited
What is my status
Am I your woman or your friend
Where do I stand
In the front or back
Can I come to your house
No I can't because you are still living with her

Keeping It Real

Can you come to my place
Of course you can
There has never been any obstacles keeping you from that
I can't even be around your family
Because no one is supposed to know about me
If you keep stringing me along, you will see
See me walk away with my head held high
Do you see me
Do you see me
There's this sign that says DO NOT ENTER
The same sign that's been in front of me for years
I've gotten stronger and have shaded less tears
Because I've limited myself from enjoying my life
By adding unnecessary strife
So now there are no limitations
Its time to be free
No one will hold me back because I'm doing this for me

Stop
Stop saying you love me
But you still live with her
Stop trying to hold on to me
When you still living in that house
Stop trying to convince me that you want to leave
Stop trying to make me believe
Everything you say is real
When I know the deal
Stop promising to give me a ring
When you're still legally bound to someone else
You can't cut the ties right now
That I know to be true
I won't hang around for another year or two
Stop saying things with her are nothing
Stop making it seem like you can't be there anymore
When opportunity is right at the door
Stop it all because it gets you nowhere
Stop it now because I cannot bear

Keeping It Real

Emotionally Spent
I'm tired of the up one day down the next
This roller coaster ride is making me dizzy
Happy one minute sad the next
I'm not happy like I used to be
This emotional ride is getting to me
Get me off this tortuous journey
When you continue saying it's about me
I'm emotionally spent broke with emotions
I want stability can you give me that
Can you give me what I deserve and not just what I want
Life with you is like an hourglass half empty half full
It's all or nothing can't you see
I am not part-time but full-time and that's how it is
No more give it more time because time is not what I have
I'm emotionally spent broke with emotions
I need a break from the agony of the side piece
You seem to take me for granted
Thinking I'm going to always be here
It has been years and that's too much time
Given away to someone who is still in a rut
My heart is big, colossal even
What can I do
Continue sitting around putting my life on hold
I'm emotionally spent broke with emotions
I need to be free
Free from all of the worry
Free to be me

Black Dodge Ram
If you've ever had a Dodge Ram that's big and rugged as can be
It acts tough, looks tough but if only you can see
The inside seems nice and clean
But really it's a smokescreen
From afar its one of the maddest trucks around shiny on the outside
But really messy on the inside

Keeping It Real

That black Dodge Ram would get up and go at all times of the day and night
It always wanted to go to Walmart and Lowe's, hell, anywhere it pleased
There were times when that truck played the best music
The kind you sing along with and hold hands to
But somewhere down the road the music played less and less
There was no more going to Walmart and Lowe's
No more drives to the movies or to get food
Black Dodge Ram would leave in the middle of the night without me
Black Dodge Ram didn't care anymore
It looked at me like I meant nothing
It didn't open or close the door for me except when it was to show off
That Dodge Ram didn't like me anymore
That truck pushed me to the side and forced me out of the door
Next thing I know it died
It didn't break down first
It quit on me because it didn't want me riding in it anymore
Black Dodge Ram was looking for someone else
So it stopped taking me to places I loved to go
Now there are other passengers in the seats
But it's okay because that 5-month ride was only temporary

2020 Danger Zone

There is this thing out there that's killing people
It's odorless, tasteless, you can't even see it
It's a danger to all mankind
You'd think it's the Devil himself
It's small and round under the microscope
It's causing people to lose their minds
It's called the danger zone because nowhere is safe
What is the cure you ask
God's mercy and saving grace
Prayer, prayer, and more prayer is what we need
To get passed this debacle and see it through
There are ones who have passed away because of this thing
We now wonder what life has to bring
If we continue to put faith in our Mighty God
Then there will be no more worrying

Keeping It Real

Her Wish
She wishes she could stop feeling the way she does
The kind of feeling of regret
She wants things back the way it was
Before she gave her whole life and heart away
To someone who won't leave his house
To someone who is legally bound to someone else
But she likes having him around
She loves this person with all her heart
She even left him alone for awhile
Just to see what mistake she made
Oh but was it a mistake because she thought her love would fade
She found out her heart screamed for him
But he doesn't belong to her
He's been leaving his home for years
And a lot of times she just shed tears
There were times she was happy and sad
But a lot of times she felt angry and mad
Mad at herself for changing positions
She wishes she looked ahead
But she looked back instead
She loves this man as you can see
So what is she going to do
Right now she wishes she had a clue

Unauthorized
What position do you play
I asked what position do you play
Oh you don't know or don't want to say
Can you go to his house
Can you go to her place
When you are sick can he visit you
Or he has to wait until she's away
Can you take care of her when she's sick
No because you're not authorized
What position are you in

Keeping It Real

First place second place
Can you comprehend
You can't do anything but wait
Wait for a phone call when he's not around
You know it's not right you tell yourself
But you put up with it anyway
Your heart is deep in it
His wife is authorized to do what she wants
Just thinking about that taunts you
You're not authorized to visit him at home
You're not authorized to see her in the hospital
You can't do a damn thing
Because of the spot you're in
You can't make any decisions because you are not the wife
You cant sit next to her while she's in bed
You can't do anything but shake your head
Yell scream talk out loud if you want
It won't change the position you are in
All you need to know is you won't win

Still Married
You say she's your baby
But you're still married
You say he's your man
But you're still married
Why can't you just understand
Nothing changes your status until you do
You say she's your future
But your ass is still married
How long have you had him waiting
A month, a year or two
Time is a precious commodity
Quit wasting hers
You keep saying you're leaving
But you are still there
You say you love him
But you are still married

Keeping It Real

Move out of the way
Give someone else a chance
Someone who has time for romance

Angry at Myself
Why did I allow you into my life
Just because we reconnected
Doesn't mean we should've stayed connected
You acted like you were interested
But you really wasn't
Angry with myself for dealing with you
Wasted my time trying to see who you are
What I saw didn't get too far
You used me as a bridge to walk to someone else
Angry at myself for looking your way
Now we don't even talk
Don't have two words to say
I hope you found what you were looking for
You can best believe it won't last
And when it doesn't don't come looking for my ass
Angry at myself but this too shall pass

Love Yourself
Tell yourself you are beautiful
Tell yourself you are handsome
Tell yourself you are smart
You're confident too
Love the skin you're in
Love everything about you
You will have good days and bad ones too
It's okay because you're still one of a kind
Look in the mirror and smile
Do this everyday and you will see
Just how much happier you will be
Love yourself and all your quirky ways
We all think we are strange at times
But that's the unique way God created us

Keeping It Real

So wrap your arms around yourself and squeeze really tight
This is what you should do for the rest of your life

Just Friends

You want to be just friends right
Then stop acting like you want more
You can't have it your way
You can't undress me with your eyes
And expect to get a prize
We are just friends so keep it that way
Don't talk about nothing else
Because I won't have nothing to say
The stereotypical issue is having your cake and eating it too
I can't be just a friend and your lover too
No kissing no touching
Nothing at all
We're just friends and that's what it will be
If you can't make up your mind
Then leave me be

What Do I Look Like

I know you are attracted to me
This is for sure
But you don't want me more than a friend
What do I look like
Just someone to feel on or kiss
What do I look like
I'm not to be used
We are just friends right
Boy don't get it confused
I may have thick thighs and a pretty face
But you will not take advantage of me
Because I will cut you off quicker than the eye can see
A lady to be hidden
Oh no no no not me
I am a diamond so shiny and bright

Keeping It Real

So back to what I said
We're just friends right
Now   what   do   I   look   like

Keeping It Real

References

"Narcissist." *The Merriam-Webster.com Dictionary*, Merriam-Webster Inc., https://www.merriam-webster.com/dictionary/narcissist. Accessed 23 November 2019.

Made in the USA
Columbia, SC
28 February 2025